Once Upon an If

Also available in the If series:

The If Machine by Peter Worley

The If Odyssey by Peter Worley

Coming soon:

The If Man by Peter Worley

Also available from Bloomsbury Education:

100 Ideas for Primary Teachers: Developing Thinking Skills by Steve Bowkett

Getting the Buggers to Think by Sue Cowley

How to be an Outstanding Primary School Teacher by David Dunn

Once Upon an If

The Storythinking Handbook

By Peter Worley

Illustrations by Tamar Levi

BLOOMSBURY

LONDON • NEW DELHI • NEW YORK • SYDNEY

808.543
WOR

Published 2014 by Bloomsbury Education
Bloomsbury Publishing plc
50 Bedford Square, London, WC1B 3DP

www.bloomsbury.com

978-1-4411-1814-1

10 9 8 7 6 5 4 3 2 1

Typeset by Fakenham Prepress Solutions, Fakenham, Norfolk NR21 8NN
Printed by CPI Group (UK) Ltd, Croydon, CR0 4YY

This book is produced using paper that is made from wood grown in managed, sustainable forests.
It is natural, renewable and recyclable. The logging and manufacturing processes conform to the
environmental regulations of the country of origin.

To view more of our titles please visit www.bloomsbury.com

Online resources accompany this book at:
www.bloomsbury.com/once-upon-an-if-9781441118141

Please type the URL into your web browser and follow the instructions
to access the resources. If you experience any problems please contact
Bloomsbury at: companionwebsite@bloomsbury.com

This book is dedicated to all the good teachers I have had the honour of meeting, being taught by or working with. I will name two:

Joan Lagden, who was my final primary school teacher. She taught with stories and said to me as I left the school that I should get back in touch with her when I had written my first book. I did.

Paula Kitson-Moore MBE, who inspired me towards a teaching career and who taught me that teaching young children matters.

I would add that very little matters more.

Contents

XII Contents

Acknowledgements

Thank you to the following people, without whom this book would not be what it is:

Holly Gardner at Bloomsbury Education; Anne Fine, for being so approachable and delivering her foreword so promptly; Philosophy Foundation specialists Andrew Day, Robert Torrington, Steve Hoggins; teachers Dylan Ross, Sue Palin; lecturer Will Rasmussen for telling me the story of Polycrates; Nigel Warburton for his lecture on 'voices in philosophy' for The Institute of Philosophy; Rick Lewis of *Philosophy Now* magazine for the expression 'they can be wrong as long as they are wrong in the right way'; Peter Adamson for his introductory lecture on Arabic philosophy; Melanie Wilson (formerly of Continuum) for her encouragement of the original idea; Grace Robinson of *Thinking Space* for allowing me to use and develop her 'concept fishing'; Tamar Levi, once again, for her wonderful illustrations and prompt delivery of them; my friend Nadine Gritten for the 'Wellington' example; Robert Fisher, E. Gary Gygax, Steve Jackson and Ian Livingstone for the books that I have identified as inspirations for this one (going back to my early school days); the many classes and teachers with whom I have been able to develop these lessons and stories; Katie, for necessary distraction. A special thanks to Oliver Leech (George Orwell and Strunk and White) for help with grammar and style.

Emma. For everything.

Foreword

In an increasingly complicated world, we more than ever want our children to be able to think with clarity, rather than lead lives hampered or derailed by all those false assumptions and unexamined prejudices that seem as easily inherited as freckles or brown eyes.

How can we go about teaching them to peel back the surface of their first thoughts on a matter, or even their strongest beliefs, and look at them with more care? It sounds a dry process till you introduce the notion of doing it through story. Fiction has always fostered the moral, intellectual and emotional development of the growing child. ('*Should* she have done that?' 'Would *I*?' 'What *else* could have been done?' 'How would it *feel*?') Good stories highlight the sheer complexity of things. They furnish a far greater understanding of the world and everyone in it. For most of us, fiction has always been the earliest – and many would argue the best – instrument we have had for ethical enquiry.

This book is here to both highlight, and offer useful advice on, every aspect of the art of telling and unpicking stories. But as we all know, some tales work better than others in this respect. The stories in *Once Upon an If* have been especially chosen or written to provoke and tease out thought, and encourage discussion, in pupils of a wide age range in the classroom setting. As the author claims, it is a book that 'uses stories to *think with* rather than to *think about*.'

'Tell me a story!' is a perennial plea and we are all of us the richer for that. This book shows clearly why.

Anne Fine, Children's Laureate 2001–03

Preface

Unlocking the reader's mind

In my line of work, as a philosophy facilitator in classrooms and elsewhere, I have become increasingly fascinated and enchanted by stories and storytelling. There are a number of excellent books describing the art of storytelling but I have been unable to find one that is both dedicated to stories as a way into thinking and also teaches the art of storytelling in a way that is approachable and manageable for any busy teacher. In my view, the best storytelling book I have had the good fortune to discover is – sadly now out of print – *Once Upon a Time: A Storytelling Handbook* by Breneman and Breneman (1983). I wanted to write something like this but with the extra dimension of showing how to use these skills for engaging thinkers, or, as science fiction writer Philip K. Dick said, for 'unlocking the reader's mind'.

This book aims to take the Breneman and Breneman book, combine it with Robert Fisher's *Stories For Thinking* (1996) and then add more than a pinch of something extra, continuing the ideas begun with the previous books in my 'If' series, *The If Machine* (2011) and *The If Odyssey* (2012).

I touched upon the art of the storyteller in *The If Odyssey,* which included a 'Storykit' section of hints and tips for the would-be storyteller. *Once Upon an If* aims to take what was only introduced in that book much further. I still see *The If Odyssey,* however, as a starting place for the storyteller and so I've threaded it through this book too and many of the examples I give are from it. Central to *The Odyssey* is *information*: who has it and how much of it they choose to divulge. Odysseus is privy to many aspects of the forthcoming journey through special means and devices, such as prophecy and gods. Much of Odysseus' difficulty comes from what he knows and whether – or *when* – he should reveal his special knowledge to the crew. The sting of this responsibility is most keenly felt with the dilemma of Scylla and Charybdis, in which Odysseus has to decide whether or not to tell his crew of the hidden monster that only he knows about. The storyteller, to some extent, shares this responsibility with Odysseus, and what shapes the storyteller and the audience's response – just as it shaped Odysseus' character – is *how* the story-teller chooses to uncover the narrative her story will reveal. How one thinks about a story will also be shaped by what information one has about it.

Many thinking programmes for children can tend towards being over-procedural. Too much procedure can run the risk of losing the children's interest. The first rule of any thinking programme is to make sure that it engages; good thinking will only happen if the thinker is properly engaged. The best way to achieve this is to include a 'wow-factor' somewhere near the beginning of the children's thinking experience. As a philosopher working in schools, I believe that the subject of philosophy has a wow-factor, and, done well, children often become helplessly engaged in philosophical discussions (whether or not they enjoy them!). Much of my previous work has been about trying to get children to start philosophising as soon as possible, thereby sidestepping the 'wow-killer' of too much procedure. But sometimes philosophy takes too long. Something is occasionally needed to produce a wow-factor straight away, to really hook them before the philosophy begins. For me, this something is very often *storytelling*. If you find the advice of this book useful and effective then turn your 'telling' (an abbreviation for 'story-telling' that I will occasionally use throughout this book that is in common usage in storytelling circles) to all other aspects of your teaching too.

Some of the stories in this book are traditional (e.g. *The Six Wise Men*) and some original (e.g. *The Promise-Slippers*). This is because I find that I can construct a story to meet what I call a 'thinking end' often more easily than finding one that fits. This experimentation allows *Once Upon an If* to contain stories that explore, question and challenge the nature of story itself. *Once Upon an If* is not just a book about thinking with and through stories. It is a book of *thinking stories*.

Introduction

Storytelling animals

'Stories distinguish us from animals more than any opposable thumb.'
Jane Yolen *Favourite Folk Tales From Around The World* (1987)

Here is an extract from the story of Sheherazad that frames the collection of stories *The Arabian Nights*:

'[Because of their infidelity] when Shahriyar returned to his palace he had the heads of his guilty servants, the maids and that of his wife chopped off and he took his own terrible revenge on womankind: each night he would take a new virgin bride, sleep with her and then have her killed, only to take another virgin bride the next night, repeating the ritual. This went on for three years, after which time many of the daughters of the city had either been killed or taken away by their terrified fathers. Shahriyar's vizier was the man charged with finding a new virgin each day until one night, he returned home and said to one of his daughters, Sheherazad, that he had not been able to find a single virgin anywhere in the city. He did not know what to do. Sheherazad then calmly said to him, 'Marry me to him father, for I believe that I may be able to change him.'

'You are not to risk your life!' he told her, 'All women think they can change their husbands, but seldom can they.'

She simply told him that it must be done. After much remonstration he eventually agreed, fearing that it would be the last he would see of his beloved daughter. Sheherazad instructed him to make sure that he send her sister Dunyazad to see them both on the evening of their wedding with instructions for Dunyazad to ask Sheherazad for a story with which to say goodbye. Sheherazad, you see, was a very good storyteller and she had spent many years finding and learning stories from anywhere she could.

After they were married Shahriyar told his wife to accompany him to his bed. They spoke together for a while until Sheherazad said, 'May I send for my sister, Dunyazad, so that I may say goodbye to her? She is very dear to me.'

'Of course you may,' said Shahriyar, 'I am not completely heartless.'

So, Dunyazad was sent for whilst Shahriyar slept with his new bride. When it came for Dunyazad to leave she said to Sheherazad, 'Please, sister, tell me a story before I go, to remember you by. Your stories are always so enchanting!'

'May I?' requested Sheherazad of her husband, 'I shall tell it to you too, if you would like,' she promised.

'You have permission. I am ready to hear a story now. Tell us both a story until the sun comes up. Then, I am afraid, you must die.'

So, Sheherazad began one of her stories as both her sister, Dunyazad, and her new husband, Shahriyar, settled down to listen. She breathed in and began...'

... and you could almost say that telling stories is what we do when we breathe out. For us, it is as necessary as breathing but more distinguishing. And by that I mean: though breathing is necessary for us to live, it's something we share with other animals. Storytelling is distinctive to our nature as human beings, it's a feature we don't share with any other animal. It is also one of our oldest practices. Marie Shedlock, the storyteller and author of the seminal 1915 book *The Art of The Story Teller*, describes it as 'almost the oldest art in the world'. We are *the storytelling chimpanzee*, or, in Terry Pratchett's formulation, *Pan Narrans* (2013). But, first, I would like to tell a story that shows the essential role stories have played in my life.

By profession I am a visiting philosophy teacher, facilitating children both in primary and secondary schools to be able to take part in philosophical discussions. With younger children (from nursery to age seven), following the lead of practitioners Joanna Haynes and Karin Muriss, I have often used picture books like *Mr Good* by Roger Hargreaves (2008) and *Frog is a Hero* by Max Velthuijs (1997).

Then, one year I was placed with a particularly challenging class of Year 2 (age six to seven) children who found it difficult to sit down at all, let alone concentrate for any prolonged period of time. When using picture books I had found that classes often became somewhat distracted; either the children couldn't see the pictures well from where they were sitting or they became so interested in the details on the page that they felt they had to tell the class. But, in the main, these distractions were manageable and, in fact, often their attention to the details would pay off later when they had to analyse the stories – and the pictures – in order to think about them and then discuss them. With this class, however, these distractions would sometimes lead to fights (verbal and/or physical) that often brought the sessions to an end. None of my tried-and-tested techniques for engaging classes seemed to work.

And then I remembered having read something in Robert Fisher's *Stories For Thinking* (1996) about learning the stories from memory and *telling* them rather than reading them. This advice appeared in just a paragraph or two in the introduction to his book, which I had been using as a resource for stories to read from to my classes, but I had remembered it. I thought I would give it a go. I learned a story and, as Fisher recommends, I wrote down a list of keywords from the story to keep next to me while I told it. I was amazed at the results. The children, who would previously not even sit down willingly, sat motionless, their faces locked onto mine as I told the story. It was as if I had cast a magic spell. I thought to myself, 'This is it! This is how I am going to get through to them.' The level of engagement was so high that I was able to get a good ten minutes of reflective discussion from them before the magic wore off.

With this class, storytelling became my *modus operandi* and each week I would prepare another story and would see if I could hold on to them in discussion for just a little while longer than the week before. Two terms later, they were able to sit and engage with the stories and with each other in discussion for – on one occasion – over an hour. Much of the success I put down to storytelling.

With that one class and in just two terms-worth of work I built up a small repertoire of stories that I would go on to use in many of my other classes too. Now, when I go into a classroom and detect concentration or behavioural problems, I tell a story. Storytelling has become my primary mode of presentation with all ages and it's never failed yet to engage and stimulate. When I am asked to give a lecture I try to find a way to present it as – or within – a story.

The lead character of the opening story in Part two: A treasury of stories, (see page 85), derives her name, Zadie, from – in my view – the Goddess or patron saint of stories: *Sheherazad*. What the story *Once Upon an If* and Sheherazad's story have in common is that they both 'frame' the collection of stories they introduce, they are both meta-stories – in other words, a story *about* stories – and both contain stories-within-stories.

Like Sheherazad, I had managed, with my difficult Year 2 class, to stay the executioner's hand, with stories. Every time I had entered this classroom – and others like it since – my head was on the block and it was stories that saved me. This book will look at the *how* and the *why* of stories, storytelling and storytelling-for-thinking.

What is in this book?

This book has two parts; the first looks at the nature of stories and how they can be used for teaching and thinking with. Key ideas introduced in this first section include: how stories can be used as a rehearsal for life-situations, and to cultivate – but not inculcate – the development of human virtues; how stories can be used to activate children as autonomous, critical agents rather than (as has been done for millennia) to pour values into children seeing them as passive vessels; how stories can be used to create controversies with which children can then think more deeply.

It goes on to look at storytelling skills and provides practical strategies for using stories to think with, such as: when in a story it is best to run an enquiry, how to use different tenses and first, second and third person perspectives to more fully engage and activate an audience; how to deal with 'the moral' of a story; how to question in a child-centred way and how to use dilemmas to jolt children into thinking more deeply. There is also a brand new and widely applicable procedure called the Concept Box for teachers to use and apply to the stories in this book but also to stories and poems outside of it too.

The second part is a treasury of stories both traditional and original, complete with lesson plans, guidance and suggestions for use with a class. Each chapter contains the age appropriateness of the story, what themes and issues are touched upon and some suggested extension activities following a similar structure to *The If Machine* and *The If Odyssey*.

Online resources

You can also access the online resources that accompany this book for supplementary materials to use with a class at www.bloomsbury.com/once-upon-an-if-9781441118141. Resources can also be found at www.philosophy-foundation.org/resources.

These include:

- Downloadable slideshow for *Once Upon an If (part one)*. (bloomsbury.com)
- Story-writing template for the '*Once Upon an If*' classroom activity. (bloomsbury.com)
- Alternative prose version of *The Luckiest Man in the World*. (bloomsbury.com)
- The Cat that Barked dialogue version. (bloomsbury.com)
- 'Thinking in pictures' – a list of picture books for thinking with, complete with task questions. (philosophy-foundation.org)

- 'More stories to think with' – a list of prose stories for storytelling complete with title, where it can be found and possible thinking themes that accompany them. (See Appendix 1 'More stories to think with' page 214). (philosophy-foundation.org)

Who is this book for?

This book is aimed primarily at teachers working with children aged seven to eleven. Not all the stories have this range, though. For instance, *It* would work well with seven-year-olds but *Sindbad and The Pit* would only be appropriate for ten and eleven-year-olds, and even then the discretion of the teacher is needed (see individual chapters for details). Many of the stories would also be ready to go with older children such as the Sindbad stories with secondary-aged children, and many others may need nothing more than a little adaptation for use with older children and also some adult audiences. The extensive Sheherazad's Handbook section (Chapter two), which lists many storytelling techniques, should be of interest to anyone who does, or would like to start, using storytelling in their work such as teachers, librarians, public speakers or CEOs, either to begin using or to develop storytelling skills.

How to use this book

1 You may, of course, read this book from cover to cover.
2 Alternatively:
   - Using the contents page to help, dip into the book and read the entry or section that interests you.
   - If necessary, follow the references to the other relevant sections and entries that will aid your understanding and/or interest.
3 Another approach is to:
   - Go to Appendix 1: 'Quick view steps' (see page 207).
   - Read through the procedures that are briefly outlined there.
   - Turn to the referenced pages that are relevant for a better understanding of the procedure.
   - Consult the Quick view steps as a structural reminder when running a session or lesson plan (you may photocopy the relevant page).
4 Finally, you may:
   - Turn to a story and read the chapter.
   - Consult Appendix 1 (see page 207) to see which procedure best suits your needs with the story you want to use.
   - Then turn to the referenced pages that are relevant for you to be able to make use of your chosen story and lesson plan.
   - Consult the Quick view steps as a structural reminder when running a session or lesson plan.

The book has been written to stand alone from the other books in the *If* series but where I have identified cross references I have noted them in brackets for those readers who have all of the books and are interested in following them up. Though I hope you will find the more philosophically-inspired entries interesting, there is no special requirement, other than personal interest, that you read the entries in the *Thought stories* section, although the ideas in this section may well inform your practice.

If you would like to develop the philosophical / critical thinking side (see 'Thinking Kit' on page 70) of this book then *The If Machine* book should be of interest to you. If you would like to turn your new-found storytelling skills to a more ambitious project – even than the Sindbad stories – then *The If Odyssey* should perfectly meet your needs. All the *If* books overlap in that they all, to a greater or lesser extent, have things to say about facilitation, philosophy, critical thinking, stories and storytelling.

Part 1
The 'How To' of Storytelling and Storythinking

Thinking about stories

What's the story to storytelling?

'Music is not in the notes but in the silence between.'
Attributed to Wolfgang Amadeus Mozart, composer.

What is a story? Any definition I attempt that aims to include all the necessary and sufficient conditions of a story will fall short in some aspect or other and I'm sure that if you think hard enough you will be able to find an example of a story that stands outside my definition, or that refutes it. Story, like poetry, art or philosophy, resists exhaustive definition. If it's definitions that you want then I suggest you take a look at Kendall Haven's *Story Proof* (2007).

I think you already know what a story is. You know that *The Three Little Pigs* is one. You know what kind of stories this book will prepare you to tell and that it will not teach you how to read, for instance, a *Haynes* car manual for the edification of your family at Christmas. (Or maybe it can?!)

Here's a very short story shakily attributed to Ernest Hemingway, and often cited as the shortest story ever written:

'For sale: baby shoes, never worn.'

First of all, is this a story? If so, why is it? Stories are often said to include, among other things, characters, detail, plot, obstacles and goals, struggles, a beginning-a-middle-and-an-end and some kind of emotional engagement (Haven, 2007). Does Hemingway's example contain, or achieve, all these?

When I first read this story to my wife, Emma, she responded with 'Oh, no!' as the tragedy (as she saw it) of the situation reached her. Hemingway is often considered a master of succinctness, so what story has he, succinctly, managed to tell in these carefully-chosen six words? I asked Emma to respond to the following questions. Here's what I asked and what she said:

- *What can you tell me about any characters there may be in the story?* 'There's a mother and / or a father.'
- *What is the plot of the story?* 'Someone has lost, or not been able to have, a baby.'
- *Are there any goals and struggles? If so, what are they?* 'The goal is to have had the baby and the struggle was, presumably, their trying to have one. It's tragic.'
- *Is the character's goal (or goals) achieved?* 'No. That's what makes it tragic.'
- *What was your emotional response to the story?* 'Sadness.'

And all this in just six words.

Key to the success of this story – and what makes *storytelling*, in my view – is not only what is written or said but also what the reader creates, what happens *between* the writer and those that read these few words. What can be learnt from this is that story is *reciprocal meaning making*. As well as any formal elements such as plot and character, any attempt to define 'storytelling' – and possibly even 'story' itself – must include the relationship between *the teller* and *the told to* and any meaning that is created between them out of that relationship. As Gregory Currie says in his book *Narratives and Narrators* (2012): 'Narratives are *intentional-communicative artefacts*'. Story – a type of narrative – is not merely content and form; it is also a kind of dance, and, as they say, it takes two:

> 'Told and retold or read and reread, the story exists neither in the mouth nor on the page, neither in the ear nor the eye. It is created between. The story is… re-created between the teller and the listener, between the writer and the reader.'
> Jane Yolen, *Favourite Folktales From Around The World* (1987)

When my wife told the Hemingway story to somebody else that other person responded very differently, reflecting her own concerns: 'It's about someone who buys things for the family but whose things are not wanted.' A very different story. This shows that when enough 'space' is left between the words of a story (also poems, plays etc.) there is so much more that the audience can – or needs to – do to finish it. Only when the reader has been engaged can the story be completed; can it be said to be a story told. What makes storytelling special in this regard is that this *in-between-ness* is spontaneous, it happens during the telling and, consequently, both affects and effects the telling, and that is what makes storytelling a living, breathing art.

Types of story

Just as story is a kind of narrative, there are many kinds of story. Here is a list of the most common, and some less common, forms that formal stories take. (This list is far from exhaustive so, by way of delimitation, I have focused on the types of story that feature in this book):

- *Myths and legends (also hero tales)* – these very often involve stories of gods and heroes and often inhabit a strange world between fiction and non-fiction, in that many of them were once thought to be true, or were founded in some truth. This idea is nicely captured in J.M.W. Turner's painting, Ulysses Deriding Polyphemus, where the cyclops features – only just – as an apparition. Apart from some obvious features such as magic and monsters, it is often difficult to know what was true and what was not in myths. Troy, for instance, was a real place; a war between the Trojans and the Greeks probably really was waged, but whether there was a wooden horse or not remains shrouded in myth as there is no evidence, beyond the oral and written narrative traditions, one way or the other.
  Myths would often fulfil the role of explaining how things came to be, such as the origin of the world itself. Legends would often describe the exploits of certain historical or fictional – and often both – characters or heroes. Myths often take place in their own universe, sometimes known as a *mythos*, that unifies the many different stories contained therein through shared laws, history and characters. Perhaps our most well-known series of myths and legends are those of the ancient Greeks and the Norse people, but there are probably as many myth-universes as there are cultures in the world. They reflect the beliefs, values and practices of the peoples that tell them at a certain time in history. An example of a modern myth-system might be the universes you find in comic-book-worlds such as the DC-universe, containing Superman and Batman among others, and the Marvel-universe, containing Spiderman and The Hulk.

- *Fables and parables (including animal stories)* – these are often told to impart a lesson or moral. Fables often contain magical or supernatural elements and parables are usually grounded in real life. Among the best known of these are Aesop's Fables (circa. Fifth Century BCE) (e.g. *The Boy Who Cried Wolf*) and the parables told by Jesus in the gospels (e.g. *The Prodigal Son*). Because of the moral they often contain these stories are more difficult for thinking, though they can be used effectively if approached with care. (See 'Stories and thinking' on page 14 in this chapter and 'Making effective use of the moral' on page 64 in Chapter three: Storythinking.)
- *Fairy tales (traditional, folk or wonder tales)* – these are traditional oral tales with elements of magic and fantasy that have been passed down through the generations and are usually associated with certain classic collections compiled at a certain time, such as the German Grimm brothers (e.g. *The Frog Prince*, *Sleeping Beauty*) see Tatar (2012) or Charles Perrault in France (e.g. *Cinderella*, *Little Red Riding Hood*) see Tatar (2002).
- *Anecdotes* – usually short stories that describe something that really happened. Good 'in the pub' storytellers and comedians often tell anecdotes. This book is peppered with anecdotes from my own experiences in the classroom to make sure that there is a strong story element to the book itself.
- *Humour stories* – jokes are not in themselves stories (such as the very short variety, e.g. Jimmy Carr's 'Venison's dear isn't it?' or 'Pretentious? Moi?') but jokes can also be stories. Like thought-experiments (see below) they are stories only in a very thin sense, using story to set up a situation for a specific purpose, either for thinking or laughing. However, there is a breed of humour story that doesn't seem to fall easily into any of the other categories but neither are they jokes (see Calvin and Hobbes in Watterson, Bill (1995) in the bibliography).
- *Short stories* – this is a literary form of story and it is not at all easy to define. A good classroom activity is to try to say exactly what the difference is between a short story, a novella and a novel. For instance, which is Joseph Conrad's *Heart of Darkness* (1899) or H.G. Wells' *The Time Machine* (1895)? And what is it that makes them one and not the other? See also *Flash-fiction*, which is a somewhat arbitrary distinction for very short stories sometimes capped at 20 words, sometimes 300 or as many as 1000 words. In the Twitter-informed age of brevity there is a growing interest in very short forms.
- *Tall tales* – closely related to anecdotes, urban myths and hero tales. They are said to be true but are most likely apocryphal, at least in the detail of the story. Tall tales are best thought of as 'exaggerations' about real events or historical figures. (See the story *Il Duomo* on page 151 for an example of a tall tale.)

- *Tales with a twist* – these stories have a surprise ending of one kind or another and are strongly associated with the author Roald Dahl after he coined the expression 'Tales of the unexpected' for his, now classic, collection of tales with a twist (see Roald Dahl's *Tales of The Unexpected* (1979)). Earlier examples include *The Necklace* (1884) by Guy de Maupassant and *The Monkey's Paw* (1902) by W.W. Jacobs. One of the earliest examples I have found is the story of *Polycrates and The Ring* from the ancient Greek historian Herodotus (included in this book as *The Luckiest Man in the World*, see page 177).
- *'What if' stories (and thought-experiments)* – 'What if sadness was against the law?', 'What if there was a magic crown that had the power to make you ruler of all the land?', 'What if, with a ring of invisibility, you could avoid being caught?' These are just some of the 'What if?' questions that lie behind the *what if?* stories *The Saddest King* (Chris Wormall, 2008), *The Magic Crown* (see page 169) and *The Ring of Gyges* (Plato circa. Fourth Century BCE), respectively. Science fiction stories are seen as *what if?* stories *par excellence*, but these stories do not need to be science fiction; magic or an imagined change in the law can allow the mind to pursue a *what if?* scenario. The term *novum* has been coined by critic Darko Suvin (1979) to describe that element which is new and that distinguishes the imagined world from our own in a *what if?* story. For example, in a story where it is supposed that human beings develop a technology enabling them to access each other's thoughts, the distinguishing *novum* in the story is the idea of technological telepathy. The *what if?* story is closely related to the more scientific thought-experiment but is distinguished from it by having a fuller narrative element; a beginning, a middle and an end (see page 17 for more on thought-experiments.) However, some stories, such as many of the stories of Philip K. Dick (see bibliography), are also thought-experiments: testing our intuitions using an imagined set of circumstances but which also tell a yarn.

Thought experiment extension activities

Where you see *'TX'* (standing for 'thought-experiment') in the questions that follow the stories in this book, I have included some thought-experiments in their barest form, purely for the purposes of thinking. But if you wanted to expand these into extension activities then you could set the class the task of writing a *what if?* story around one of these nova. Or, you could try the exercise for yourself as a story to read or tell to your class for thinking with. The technological telepathy example above could be used in this way.

As if: truth and lies in fiction

Here's a Sudanese storyteller's opener:

> 'I'm going to tell a story
> It's a lie.
> But not everything in it is false.'
>> From Norma J. Livo and Sandra Rietz *Storytelling Process and Practice* (1986)

And here is an extract from the *Stanford Encyclopaedia of Philosophy*'s entry on *holes*:

> 'Naive… descriptions of the world treat holes as objects of reference, on a par with ordinary material objects… yet it might be argued that reference to holes is just a [way of speaking], that holes are mere… *as-if* entities, fictions.' (See bibliography)

I am often asked by children who hear the stories I tell, 'Is it true?' And it is not easy to know how to answer this question. In the dictionary, a storyteller is described as 'a reciter of tales', but the very next entry is, 'a liar, fibber'. Roger D. Abrahams (1983) said that 'tales are, in the ears of their hearers, permissible lies'. There is a school of thought that objects to the way stories are, allegedly, used to tell lies. Myths are an example of the sort of thing these objectors have in mind, and the story of Santa Claus, to this day, divides parents over whether it should be told as true or not. What is so difficult about answering such a simple question as 'Is it true?'?

According to Gregory Currie (2012) the reason it is so difficult to answer is because narratives 'represent as true' the content of that narrative. But, he says, representing-as-true must be kept separate, conceptually, from being-committed-to-truth. It is true, *in the story* of Sindbad for instance, that Sindbad lands on an island that is in fact a giant turtle, and the storyteller certainly refers to the story – like a hole – *as if* it were true. But if the person who told the story were asked, outside the context of storytelling, whether they believed that the events they had described really happened, they are likely to say 'no', though perhaps with some qualification.

If the storyteller were to simply answer the question 'Is it true?' with 'No' then they would jeopardise the authenticity of their telling that is so important to the storyteller and their audience. It jeopardises the all-important *suspension of disbelief*. With adults, the suspension of disbelief is an important ironic attitude they are able to adopt in order to enter into the story-world of a particular narrative. Rationally, they know that the events they are witnessing never took place, or at least not exactly as they are told in the story, and that the characters do not exist and are not really feeling pain and the like. But, with the suspension of their disbelief, they are able to allow real emotional responses to occur in themselves.

With children, however, the picture is more complicated because their position is not necessarily ironic; sometimes, instead of a *suspension of disbelief* it may simply be *belief*. It is this sensitivity that a storyteller needs to be aware of. To illustrate this, here's another anecdote:

I used to run a session for classes based around the curriculum subject 'Earth, Sun and Moon' in which I would go into the class and tell them that I was a member of the Flat Earth Society, or FES, and I would say that, 'as a member of FES we believe that the Earth is flat and not round'. I would then use this premise to galvanise the class to try to prove to me that the Earth is round and not flat, given that they thought my 'FES position' ridiculous. This helped them to see the difficulties in proving their 'obviously true' position and it helped them see that most of the evidence they have for the Earth being round is *secondary evidence* and not *primary evidence* (also an area of the curriculum at that time).

I would always feel somewhat uncomfortable telling them that I was a member of FES when in fact I was not. My discomfort was heightened when, after the session, the children would come up to me and quiz me quite earnestly about the Flat Earth Society. I realised that the irony enjoyed by both myself and the class teacher was not shared, or even recognised, by the children. Later I adapted the session (see page 143) by telling classes a story about a time-travelling scientist in which the children were to play the role of the scientist. In the story, the scientist travels back to the time of the ancient Egyptians, who believed that the Earth was flat. I then role-played the Egyptian whilst they, playing the modern-day scientist, tried to convince me of the Earth's roundness. In doing this I felt much more comfortable because the children knew that *I* did not hold the views I espoused throughout the session even though they spoke to me during the session *as if* I did. The former situation describes what seems to me to be an *impermissible lie* and the latter, *permissible*.

Rehearsal for life

The educator Maria Montessori was one of those who had concerns about teaching children through fictional situations such as talking animals and magic. She thought that children learn best – and, indeed, prefer to learn, according to her – through real-life situations. However, there is a sense in which stories, fictional or non-fictional, provide an excellent learning context. They provide a context in which children *rehearse real life*, and they do this through the exercise of what is known as conditional, counterfactual thinking; what, in my first book *The If Machine*, I called *if-ing*. Conditional sentences or thoughts are of the following structure, 'If… then…' such as in the following sentence, 'If I want a cup of tea, then I must boil the kettle'. Counterfactuals are conditional sentences or thoughts that depict the world in a way other than how it is, such as 'If time travel were possible then it may be possible to meet oneself'. *Possible worlds* are counterfactual situations or states of affairs that are possible but not true.

Alison Gopnick (2009), has suggested that it is through fiction that children practise putting together causal pictures of the world by creating fictional, possible worlds. She says:

> 'If causal knowledge and counterfactual thinking go together, then this might explain how young children have the parallel ability to generate counterfactuals and to explore possible worlds. If children understand the way things work, they should be able to imagine alternative possibilities about them.'

In one class where I had delivered some of *The Odyssey* stories for philosophy discussions, one of which was the story of the monsters Scylla and Charybdis, a puzzled boy said, 'I don't see the point of discussing these stories because: what have monsters got to do with real life?' His classmates answered his question on my behalf adequately enough for me to have no need to. 'There might not be monsters in the real world but you still might have to make difficult decisions and this gets you thinking about that,' one girl said. Another girl, called Charlotte, said, 'It's not really about monsters, it's about choices'. Given that I had used the story to explore dilemmas, she had nailed it. The storyteller, Elizabeth Nesbitt, wrote:

> 'Story-telling provides the opportunity to interpret for the child life forces which are beyond his immediate experience, and so to prepare him for life itself.'
>
> Elizabeth Nesbitt, 'Hold on to that which is good' *The Horn Book Magazine* (1940)

Telescope of the imagination

In the groundbreaking 1973 television documentary *The Ascent of Man* Jacob Bronowski offered his own interpretation of the cave paintings made by early man. He uses a metaphor of a 'telescope of the imagination' through which the cave painters looked through to the future, imagining dangers they would come to face, while we look back as we try to understand the cave painters' story left for us on the wall of the cave.

Like the cave paintings, stories enable us to look back to the past in order to help prepare for the future. When children hear the stories of Odysseus, for example, they are preparing how they will respond to similar situations they may, one day, face. At some point in their lives the children are very likely to face a dilemma – if they haven't already. At some point they will love and lose and at some point they may have to consider the ethics of war. In science fiction we look forward often both to prepare for the future and to consider the present, or even the past. Stories are a telescope of the

imagination with which we, like the Roman god Janus, look both backwards and forwards.

Stories, though themselves fiction, are yet 'true' in that they represent the true archetypes of human actions and experiences. Charlotte again: 'It's not really about monsters, it's about choices'. So, to return to the insistent class-member's question: 'Is it true?' Well, in a way 'yes' and in a way 'no'. I shall – rather mischievously – leave it to you to decide how to answer, beyond what I have said here.

Ethics through narrative

'When I perform actions, engage in conversations and other human transactions, I am a character in a narrative of which I am in part the author.'

Bernard Williams, philosopher, from *Life As Narrative* (2009)

Consider the following dilemma:

You are the captain of a ship. Many of your men have been captured and imprisoned by a hostile force on an island. Your options are either to leave the island, thereby securing the safety of yourself and the remaining men, or to attempt to retrieve the captured men through great risk to yourself. One of your closest officers recommends that you leave the island as soon as possible as he says the odds are stacked against success in rescuing the captured men. What should you do?

One approach to this, based on duty, would have us ask: *what does (moral) duty say that I should do?* Another approach, based on consequences, has us ask: *what would produce the best outcome or the greatest amount of happiness?* You may want to answer these questions as best you can and compare how you answer them. Do your answers to the two questions differ? If so, in what way? Also ask yourself which of the two approaches appeals to you most. Why?

A person interested in developing the right virtues would ask: *what choice would make me the kind of person I think I should be?* Or, *what choice would cultivate the right kind of virtues?* How would you answer this question in relation to the dilemma above? Again, *compare and contrast* with your answers to the previous two questions.

The virtue of stories

What kind of qualities am I talking about when I talk about virtues? Lists of virtues vary but philosopher Andre Comte-Sponville (2002) has attempted to reduce them to the following central virtues:

- fidelity
- prudence
- temperance
- courage
- justice
- generosity
- compassion
- mercy
- gratitude

- humility
- simplicity
- tolerance
- purity
- gentleness
- good faith
- humour
- love.

When asked to answer the questions above to the dilemma I put to you, you may have wanted to know the answers to further questions: 'What sort of captain?'; 'What sort of ship?'; 'What is the nature of my relationship with the men? Trust? Distrust?'; 'Do I have duties elsewhere? If so, to whom?' etc. Actually, the situation described is from *The Odyssey*: the captain is Odysseus; the officer, Eurylochus, who witnessed the men captured and turned into pigs by the sorceress Circe. Odysseus is the king of Ithaca and husband of Penelope and father to Telemachus. Later, Eurylochus will disobey him and secure the destruction of the entire crew, though this last fact will only be known to someone who knows the entire story.

Do these considerations impact on your decision? How much does context really matter?

Like holes, what stories do, when it comes to ethics and virtue, is present to their audience a situation *as if* it were real and *as if* it really matters. In traditional storytelling the audience is not often enlisted to solve the problem or to respond to the dilemma as a moral agent but simply to view, as a passive onlooker, the story's unfolding. The ethical outcome for the audience here is nothing more than to learn something from what Marie Shedlock called 'the career of the hero' (Shedlock, 1915). But through the problems, dilemmas and difficulties that beset the hero there is an opportunity to *activate* the moral and ethical considerations of the audience. Not only does this provide an opportunity to practise and apply ethical thinking, it also provides a narrative context in which to do so, making the considerations as contextually near to reality as it is possible to do, short of their being real.

The narrative context includes complex situations containing many salient variables but it also – crucially – contains *relationships with others*. Stories suggest that relationships *must* play a role in how an agent approaches a dilemma. This means that stories meet a common criticism of contemporary ethics: that it is too *subjective* and *individualistic*. A narrative approach to ethics is concerned with how the ethics of the individual – what *I* should do – reaches out towards others. And this it does when life is understood narratively. As the philosopher Martha Nussbaum has written:

> 'Moral knowledge is not simply intellectual grasp of propositions; it is not even intellectual grasp of particular facts; it is perception. It is seeking a complex, concrete reality in a highly lucid and richly responsive way; it is taking in what is there, with imagination and feeling.'
>
> Martha Nussbaum, Love's Knowledge (1990)

Stories are about virtue because they are about intersecting characters in situations that call for certain, specific, human qualities. Stories are just one way that we are able to sharpen our own character in order to prepare for the narratives we will one day find ourselves in as the story of our life unfolds before, around and within us.

Stories and thinking

Received and operational beliefs

It is well known that stories form the basis of a moral education in many societies now and a long way into the past. Just think of Aesop's fables, the parables of the Bible and the Greek myths. Marie Shedlock, in her book *The Art of The Storyteller* (1915), lists at the beginning a series of storytelling aims. They include the development of dramatic joy; a sense of humour and the imagination. She also says:

> 'To correct certain tendencies by showing the consequences in the career of the hero in the story (Of this motive the children must be quite unconscious and there should be no didactic emphasis).'

And then:

> 'To present by means of example, not precept, such ideals as will sooner or later be translated into action.'

She is right to suggest that children learn best through example and respond less well to didactic instruction of moral precepts. Children can very well recite that they should not hit someone back – in other words, *received beliefs* (Fisher, 2003) – and they will do so when they understand that to be what the teacher expects to hear. But in the playground they will often hit back and when asked why, they will defend themselves with a heartfelt, 'But (s)he hit me first!' – in other words, the beliefs they act upon, or, their *operational beliefs* (Fisher, 2003). She is also right to notice that much of the value of stories lies in how the story offers the children an opportunity to rehearse for life (see page 10 for more on this).

Where I depart from Shedlock is where she says, 'Of this motive the children must be quite unconscious'. Of course, children will not always be conscious of what they take away from a story. But where one is actively seeking to morally shape the children's worldview covertly, we must beware!

The philosopher Plato from the Fifth Century BCE voiced his own concerns about how the stories of the ancient Greek gods were used to misinform and mis-shape children's minds. He was particularly concerned about how they directed children's attention away from truth. Plato also offers some of the earliest examples of stories being used for critical engagement and not for instruction, though – it should be pointed out – not with the aim of being used with children.

His most well-known book *The Republic* is dotted with stories, scenarios, myths and allegories. One of the most famous and well-used is the story of 'The Ring of Gyges' in which a shepherd finds a ring of invisibility with which he can perpetrate wicked acts and escape accountability. Plato, or so he says, draws upon an already established legend rather than invent the story in order to engage his readers with a philosophical problem. The problem he wanted to explore was: *for what reasons do we act well?* It is of course possible that we only act well in order to escape punishment, so Plato used the story to help remove the punitive element of our motivation to act in order to bring his readers to consider whether there were any reasons to act well, other than to escape punishment or receive reward. So, *if you know that you will not be caught following a chosen and wicked course of action, are there any reasons to restrain yourself from following it?*

I have run this session with children of age seven and up for many years using the lesson plan that can be found in *The If Machine*. But what is particularly interesting is the way in which the children begin to formulate their own arguments for why they should act well when left to reason it through for themselves. Rather than being given a set of unsupported precepts that they are expected to follow because they have been told to, they instead construct for themselves much more robust positions for which they give reasons why it is better to act well. These reasons range from 'it would be difficult to live with the guilt' to 'you will be *happier* doing good'. The key point is that these reasons have issued from the children themselves during discussions where they have had to defend their arguments against challenges from within the group; challenges such as 'If you can't get caught then you can do anything, can't you?'

Because the children have a greater degree of ownership over these positions, the reasons they come up with are therefore likely to leave a much greater imprint on them and have an impact on their actions. What we find here, and in contrast to Shedlock's suggestion, is that it is precisely because of the conscious engagement with the questions Plato raised that the children start to impact on their own behaviour. But, just as Shedlock says, 'there should be no didactic emphasis'.

'Thinking with' and 'thinking about'

There is an important division between two ways of approaching stories for thinking: a) where the story offers a 'way in' to a thinking issue, as with the story of Gyges above, and b) thinking about the story itself, interpreting its meanings, symbolism and assumptions etc., bringing such perspectives as psycho-analytic, Marxist, feminist insights to an exegesis of the text itself. An example of this kind of question is: *What do you think the role of women / girls in this story is supposed to tell us about the expectations of women / girls in society at that time?* The first kind of approach is accessible to all and is easily adaptable to the primary classroom. The second is much more sophisticated and, though it does not entirely exclude primary-aged children (they may raise questions like this themselves), it is much more difficult to use purposefully with that age-group. However, this second approach becomes much more appropriate for secondary-aged children or adults.

The focus of this book is the first approach to thinking with stories, using stories to provide a 'way in' to a thinking issue. The narrative itself provides the conditions that create the problem that leads the audience to consider. Put simply, this book uses stories to *think with* rather than to *think about*.

In the preface of *The If Odyssey* I said:

> 'the position of this author is not to use storytelling to instil values, as they have been used for millennia, but to critically engage an audience. The listeners are encouraged to respond and react, to become active participants in the generation of what it is they are to get from the

stories, not passive vessels for the stories to fill with received opinions and values.'

This applies as much to this book as to the previous one but I would like to add something. It is commonly believed that if one is trying to avoid using stories to moralise then one should avoid books with clear moral lessons and make use of more ambiguous, morally complex stories. And, though there are a good deal more such books on the market than there were in the past that are of a high literary quality (see Haynes and Murris, 2012), one should not overlook the often more traditional stories with morals at the end. In fact, if the aim is to engage readers critically then it would be morally remiss to censor children's reading in this way. Two simple, general questions that invite a class to start doing this are as follows: 1) 'What do you think the story is trying to teach us?' and 2) 'Do you agree with the book?' (See 'Making effective use of the moral' on page 64 for more on tackling stories with morals from a critical point of view and 'More stories to think with' Appendix 1 page 214 and online).

Stories and thought-experiments

Given that I have already mentioned 'thought-experiments' – and will do so again – I thought it germane to say a word or two about what this slightly technical-sounding term describes.

A thought-experiment (sometimes abbreviated to TX in this book) is a device used primarily by philosophers (but also scientists) to isolate and manipulate certain conceptual variables for the purposes of thought. They are sometimes also known as *intuition pumps* because of the way thought-experiments test our intuitions. One girl, in a session I was running, said that harming someone is always wrong, and many of the others in the class agreed with this; in other words, they shared this intuition. Then a girl called Yasmin said, 'but if you're in a relationship and you've got to break up with them then you have to hurt them'. Yasmin had used an imagined – but plausible – scenario to test the intuition that harming someone is always wrong. Many of the children revised their opinion about this in light of her 'test'.

Thought-experiments use this same everyday principle but often push the imagination much further out into the hypothetical, similarly testing our intuitions against imagined, relevantly plausible scenarios.

Concepts

Simply put, concepts are to do with ideas and experience. When thinking together we are trying to articulate, understand and explore the ideas and experiences we have both as individuals and as a group. Many of the ideas we have stay in our own realm of thought and experience but when we think together we share the ideas we have about something and try to make sense of those ideas together. Just like the concepts we may be thinking about, such as *fairness*, *freedom*, *meaning* and the like, the concept of *concept* is far from being free of controversy itself, so it would be wrong to try to give a simple or exhaustive definition without saying that there is a great deal more that can be said about this.

To get started, I find it helpful to think of concepts as being like the building blocks and hinges of thought, or, that which gives structure to our thinking. An idea is not necessarily the same thing as a concept, as an idea may contain many concepts: the idea of a *square*, for instance, contains further concepts such as *space*, *side*, *right-angle*, *equal* and so on. If someone has an idea for a book in which a man meets an earlier self through the medium of time travel, it is an idea that has many concepts. What creates confusion is that in common parlance the expression 'concept' is used to mean the same as 'idea', as in 'the general concept of the book is that he meets an earlier self through the medium…'

There is even a story to challenge the concept of concept: *Funes The Memorious* by the Argentinian writer J. L. Borges (2000); a *what if?* story that attempts to see through the following question: *What if someone remembered everything?*

Wrong in the right way

Thought-experiments are designed to force us to consider an idea conceptually, so how the situation is presented is not so relevant. However, it can be an obstacle to the conceptual thinking if the thinkers do not accept the conceivability of the thought-experiment. One way around this is to give the thought-experiment some scientific plausibility, or as Suvin (1979) says, make it 'cognitively logical'. This does not mean that the story need be fully scientifically explicable, demonstrable or even possible, just that the audience 'buy into it'. Here are three ways that thought-experiments are traditionally brought about for the purposes of thinking through consequences and implications. Make use of whichever device you need to in order to allow your audience to access the thinking conceit:

- *Magic*: this enables us to consider just about anything and young children have no problems suspending their disbelief when considering ideas 'within the story'. So, if the intuition is: '*fair* is getting what you want' then a magic genie can be invoked to make it the case that someone 'gets what they want' in order for the class to think through, or 'test', whether this results in *fairness* (see *The Fair Well* on page 137).

- *Science fiction*: this helps to give the scenario some conceivable plausibility. Imagine Leonardo Da Vinci asking someone to entertain the possibility of human flight by getting them to project their imagination to a time in the future when human flight has been achieved. Just because something is not currently possible does not mean that it will remain so. Time travel, longevity, artificial intelligence may all be the 'flight' of our futures. However, in a thought-experiment the conceit in question (for example, time travel) may not need to *ever* be true – or even possible – for it to function successfully in the relevant, *conceptual* way (for example, see *Flat Earth* on page 143).

- *Everyday experience*: sometimes nothing too extraordinary is needed for a thought-experiment; all that may be needed is for us to imagine something perfectly conceivable in our own everyday experience, such as the example from Yasmin earlier (see page 17). Sometimes unlikely but plausible situations are needed to test an intuition. So, if the intuition is that *writing* is simply the correct arrangement of letters then the following plausible but unlikely thought-experiment could be used to test it: imagine you tipped out some spaghetti letters on to your toast and the letters happened to spell 'eat me'. Can your food write? Is this writing? What is writing if this isn't?

2 Sheherazad's handbook: how to tell stories

The virtues of storytelling

Among the many media for telling stories such as film, literature, theatre and song, storytelling has its own – some unique – set of virtues.

Direct communication

Oral storytelling is one of the most direct forms of communication, especially between the teller and his audience. Even the written word, which is often thought of as a pure form of storytelling, is less direct than oral storytelling – a text is a *physical* barrier and the words spoken are not those of the teller but of some distant, non-present other.

For teachers, it is always tempting to defer to some kind of technology when using a story with children, whether it be a CD, DVD, interactive whiteboard or even the printing press, and there are clear advantages to using technology, but the advantages of communicating directly with your class in the kind of way that storytelling affords cannot be overstated. Here, again, we can invoke the *breath* metaphor because storytelling is a way of communicating that 'breathes'. This has a literal sense too as a teacher tells a story using nothing other than her body and vocal instrument.

Improvisation and embellishment

Once a novel, poem, play or symphony has been written then it is usually thought that, in order to best communicate the story it tells, the words, notes and phrases chosen by its author or composer should be preserved as closely as possible. Many other skills are brought to a successful production or reading such as acting, direction and reading skills; cuts are sometimes made, particularly in plays, but very rarely are changes made to the text. Actors do not rewrite scripts. Storytelling is different. The same story may be told differently by different tellers and, indeed, the same story may be told differently by the *same* teller on different occasions. In the classroom this makes a great deal of resources available to an age-group that would otherwise not have access to them (see 'Matching the register to adapt' on page 40).

Moving 'the walls'

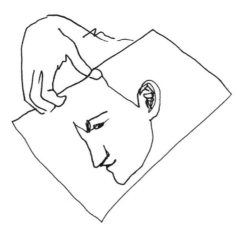

Sometimes known in theatre as 'the fourth wall' there is an invisible, metaphorical wall that lies between the actors on a stage and the audience. Actors sometimes talk about 'breaking the fourth wall'. This is done during a soliloquy, for instance, but not during a monologue, because a soliloquy in some way addresses the audience, whereas a monologue does not.

A storyteller addresses the audience throughout a telling but can, with greater freedom, play with where 'the walls' are in relation to the audience. A storyteller can, as with theatre, put the wall between him or herself and the audience, or he can point to the space behind the audience, when describing the entrance of a monster, for example. Here the wall between the events of the story and the audience has, in some way, been dissolved altogether. The audience is now inside the story but would be unseen by the characters. However, even this can change.

Varying perspectives

When a class, based on what we had done, was describing what philosophy is one Year 3 girl (age seven) said, 'In philosophy you take us *into* the stories.' At first I thought this was meant merely to say that *I tell them stories* and that perhaps she meant that I told them well, but when I questioned her further it turned out that she meant something more specific – and much more interesting. She had observed that I had been telling some of the stories in *the second person* and, if not the second person, then I had been asking them to imagine that they were a character in the story in order to explore a dilemma, for example. As we shall see, much can be made, in storytelling, by the different perspectives the storyteller, and in some cases the audience, are able to assume.

The omnipresent narrator

The storyteller is also able to inhabit different places within a story. Not just perspectives but also physical spaces. The storyteller is an omnipresent narrator who may assume different characters or points of view at any point in his telling to inform or beguile his audience.

How to tell a story

The last time I had seen a particular Year 5 class the previous year I had told them *The Odyssey* stories. Now they were in Year 6, and I was about to start a new philosophy programme with them. I began by asking them whether they had told any of the stories they had heard during *The Odyssey* sessions to anyone else. Many of the children put up their hands and told me which story (or stories) they had told and to whom. Then, one boy, called Billy, said, 'Well, I didn't really *tell* the stories; I just said what happened.' Billy had drawn a very important distinction between narrative and story that anyone about to engage in storytelling should be made aware of. So, how does one 'tell a story' rather than merely 'say what happened'?

In short, the storyteller inhabits the story and breathes life into it, making the story live for its audience so that the story is happening before them instead of being reported as having happened. How this is done is the subject of this part of the book and there are many techniques for making stories breathe.

The Goldilocks Principle

'And then she went to the porridge of the Little, Small, Wee Bear, and tasted that; and that was neither too hot, nor too cold, but just right…'
Robert Southey, *The Story of The Three Bears* (Tatar 2002)

The secret of the good storyteller (or, in my view, a good *anything*) will often have something to do with a sense of *balance*. The good storyteller uses description, but not too much, she chooses interesting words, but not too many and she will make use of movement, but not excessively. Beyond saying that the storyteller applies a sense of when and when not to use certain techniques, it is difficult to say precisely how this balance is achieved and it is this difficulty – to put a formula to it – that lifts a craft to an art; perhaps it is just this difference that *makes* something an art.

To make a musical analogy, all musicians learn, as part of their craft, techniques such as *vibrato* but it is for each musician to make his own judgements and decisions about when to apply *vibrato* and how much to apply. Any musician can learn to read music but there's an art in how to shape a phrase. There is no formula or algorithm for artistic decisions and that's what, in my view, separates art from craft.

My first use of stories for teaching thinking involved simple thought-experiments. These involved no description or fleshed-out characters and when I first learned about using description to create an atmosphere I saw the effect this had on a class, so naturally, I wanted to employ this device. Understandably, I over-used it. This is perfectly forgivable at the initial stages of learning a new technique but remember that the best storytellers are as aware of when *not* to do something as much as they are when to do it.

On the subject of appropriateness, style and taste in general, I would like to share something that neatly captures the principle I am trying to describe. George Orwell closes his seminal essay on style in writing, 'Politics and The English Language' (1946) with this short list of style points, the last one capturing the difficulty of judgement and the pitfalls involved in any attempt to provide a formula to style (my italics):

1 Never use a metaphor, simile or other figure of speech which you are used to seeing in print.
2 Never use a long word where a short one will do.
3 If it is possible to cut out a word, always cut it out.
4 Never use the passive where you can use the active.
5 Never use a foreign phrase, a scientific word or a jargon word if you can think of an everyday English equivalent.
6 *Break any of these rules sooner than say anything outright barbarous.*

How to begin and end a story

First of all, make sure you *know* exactly how you will begin and end your story. This is often the one part of the story that you will need to rehearse and learn by heart. The flow that you hope to reach in your storytelling, where you achieve fresh talk (see page 28) without reciting word-for-word, is likely to prove most elusive at the start of your story. One way is to reach for tried-and-tested sentence-starters such as 'Once upon a time…' but you need to be careful with these kinds of openers. A sentence-starter such as this will certainly trigger a certain kind of expectation from your audience: that they are about to hear a story. With young children this can be a very helpful way to signal to them that from the moment they hear these words they are engaging in a special kind of transaction with the storyteller; from that moment on the rules have changed. However, 'Once upon a time…' is in danger of sounding clichéd or trite to older children and this can be off-putting for them.

Often the best way to start a story is to start straight away with a simple statement such as 'There was once a king and he had two sons'. Some story-tellers have a preamble before starting a story, perhaps contextualising the story within their own personal experience. This can function to signpost for the audience what to look out for in the story or what lesson to draw from it. However, when using stories for thinking, avoid preambles that prefigure learning outcomes, especially moral ones. Let the story place the situations before your audience in its own way and then allow your audience to respond to it without any expectation from you about how they should do so. If using a Task Question then do not have an expectation about how they should respond to it. Try to *show* with your story and not *tell*, as the saying goes. (See 'Making effective use of the moral' on page 64 and 'Stories and thinking' on page 14 for more on dealing with morals in stories.)

If the stories are continuous or part of an ongoing narrative, such as *The Odyssey, The Voyages of Sindbad*, or – for that matter – *The Arabian Nights* then you would do well to use Sheherazad's technique of finishing on a cliff-hanger. My preferred way of doing this is to move to the very beginning of the next story, so, instead of finishing when they make their escape from one island, go on a little more until the ship hits the shore of another island; but make it arrive at night so that they can't see what sort of island it is… they'll just have to wait until next week for that! If you've been telling well, this usually elicits a disappointed 'Ohhh!' from the class as they realise that *that's it for this week!* (One of the only times a sound of disappointment is the mark of your success!)

Always leave a silence at the end of your story for your audience to take in what's happened or to readjust to reality. Whatever you do, refrain from jumping in with comments or from filling the silence until they have said something. That's like a comedian who laughs at his own jokes. (Watch comedians like Paul Merton, Jack Dee or Rich Hall who have made it almost a trademark to keep an absolutely straight face after they've delivered a joke.)

Tenses

The default tense of written stories is the past tense and this is the tense most children will be familiar with and comfortable reading. Apart from a few notable exceptions, stories *written* in the present tense read awkwardly for children. However, stories *told* in the present tense seem much more natural. This observation highlights the difference between *storytelling* and other media for communicating narratives, such as books. If you were to read it, you'd expect to see the following:

King Midas was a king who loved, more than almost anything in the whole world, gold.

But if you tell it, it would seem natural to say (albeit not to read):

'King Midas is a king who loves, more than almost anything in the whole world, gold.'

When storytelling I like to think of the past tense as being like black-and-white and the present tense like colour. The present tense (as well as the first and second person) is one way to bring the story as close to your audience as possible.

Nowness

Breneman and Breneman (1983) describe a quality they call 'nowness': '…
though [the events of the story] may have occurred hundreds of years ago,
[the story] seem[s] to come alive *now* for the audience as it hears the story.'
Although I think this quality or state can be enhanced or achieved with the
help of the present tense (and possibly the use of the first / second person) it
is important not to identify nowness with the present tense. A good storyteller
will give an audience an impression of nowness whether they tell the story in
the present or past tense, first, second or third person.

(For more on tenses see page 79 in Chapter three: Storythinking.)

Persons – first, second or third?

The second person – putting the audience into the story

Storytellers sometimes invite the audience into the story by giving them a
role. When I tell *The Odyssey*, for some of the stories, I tell the story like so: '…
you see a huge creature lumber into the cave blocking *your* way out…', in other
words, I tell it from the crew's point of view, the children inhabiting the role
of the crew. This helps to heighten the drama when they are trapped in the
cave with the Cyclops or when they are swept away from their homes in the
story *Aeolus and The Bag of Winds*. Once the audience becomes a member of
the cast then they can interact with the characters – the Cyclops sniffs around
them when he is searching for the men in the cave.

Point of view and sympathy

'Point of view' is the perspective through which the story is viewed. A great
deal may hinge on this. How the story is interpreted to the audience may
have a lot to do with who is experiencing the story. When you tell a story in
the third person and in the past tense sometimes it may not be so clear from
whose point of view the story is being relayed and so consequently it is not
clear with whom the audience are to sympathise.

One eight-year-old girl, when hearing the tale of *The Wooden Horse of Troy*
and after I had asked the question 'Were the Greeks right to go to war against
the Trojans?', said to me, 'Whose side are we on?' This was a great question
because she had implied that our emotional response to the story and how we
invest in it depends on whose side we feel we are on. But the way I had, quite

deliberately, told the story had left this somewhat ambiguous. The Greeks had done some – arguably – despicable things, such as slaughtering the Trojans while they slept, and tricking their way to a victorious conclusion to the war, but Odysseus seemed to be the hero of the story, though he too had done some questionable things. Putting the story into a first person perspective, such as Odysseus', would very likely have influenced her answer to her own question; our sympathies naturally fall with the speaker in first person stories.

So, which perspective do you adopt when telling a story? As you may already have guessed the answer depends very much on the story you wish to tell and the sympathies you wish to engender. Sometimes it will be easy to switch the perspective so that you can tell it from different perspectives with different audiences but other times the story will demand a particular perspective. The story of *The Odyssey* can be told from either perspective without too much trouble. Homer also tells it from both: the classic monster tales are told by Odysseus to King Alcinous in the first person whereas the majority of the rest of the story is told in the third person with one very curious move to the second person with the story of Eumeus, Odysseus' banished servant, suggesting that the whole tale is being told to Eumeus by Homer.

Extension activity: the Rashomon effect

The story that the musical *Wicked* tells (Maguire, 1995) is the well-known story of *The Wizard of Oz* (Baum, 1900) but from the point of view of the Wicked Witch, having the effect that the audience's sympathies lie with her. Japanese director Akira Kurosawa's film *Rashomon* (1950) is well known for telling a story from multiple perspectives and, today, the expression 'the Rashomon effect' describes the problem of establishing truth in story-telling given that stories are often (or perhaps always) irreducibly told from someone's perspective.

1 As with *Wicked* set the class the task of retelling a classic tale but from one of the other character's points of view, such as *The Three Billy Goats Gruff* but told from the Troll's point of view.
2 Or, as with the film *Rashomon*, ask them to tell the same story from several points of view. For example, Rumpelstiltskin from the point of view of:
   • The miller's daughter
   • Rumpelstiltskin
   • The King
   • The miller
   • (More challenging) the messenger.

(For more on person-perspective see 'Bite and sting: tense and person for thinking' page 79 in Chapter three: Storythinking.)

Speaking and 'lifting from the page'

Take some time to listen to, for example, the presenters of *The Today Programme* (BBC Radio 4) in the mornings. Listen to how they introduce a topic or news piece. Every so often you will hear them trip over a word. When this happens you are suddenly acutely aware that they are, at least some of the time, reading. Though I am drawing your attention to mistakes they make I do so in order to draw your attention to their skill. It is only when they make a mistake that you realise what it is they manage to achieve the majority of the time. They are able to produce the effect of speaking spontaneously though reading. This is a phenomenon the sociologist Erving Goffman (1981) called 'fresh talk' and he wrote that only the 'hyper-fluent' are able to read while making it appear spontaneous.

Try it. Select a passage from a story and read it so that it sounds like the words are falling from you naturally and not being read. Clearly distinguish between voices in any dialogue and look up from the page at your (probably imaginary) audience as you read. The best way to assess your success at this is to record yourself and then listen to the recording some time later. Does it sound read? If you were a presenter on the radio, would you know (if you were also the audience) that you were reading?

This ability to fresh talk is central to the storyteller's art whether reading or not. It must feel and sound like the words are yours and that you are thinking of them there and then. Sometimes, even though the teller is not reading, it can still sound like a recitation. So, the danger of sounding as if one is reading is not necessarily overcome with the act of memorisation. Again, once you have learnt a story, record yourself delivering it, and then wait some time before listening back to it. Does it sound recited?

When it no longer sounds as if read, though it may be, and when it no longer sounds recited, though it may be, then you will have succeeded in 'lifting the story from the page' and you will have found a way to place the story before your audience as something happening and unfolding before them. You will have achieved a sense of 'nowness' (see page 26) and brought breathed-life into the story. This could be said to be the aim of all storytelling. How you learn to lift a story from the page has much to do with how you decide to learn your stories (see 'Learning stories' on page 33).

All this applies also to stories that you decide to read to your class from books or a computer. A good exercise to try is to take a simply written children's book such as *Not Now, Bernard* by David McKee (1980) and read it as well as possible: create clearly distinguished voices for each character, including the narrator, and switch between them effortlessly; leave space between each complete thought but maintain a rhythm and flow that will carry an audience with it. In short, make it breathe.

The story *Matilda, The Fireless Dragon* has been written to be read, so use this one to practice storytelling while reading. Here are some hints for telling well while reading:

- Look at your audience as often as possible.
- Glance at a sentence and then look up towards your audience to deliver it.
- As much as possible, look down only with your eyes in order to maintain an audience-directed body and face. (A well-placed computer screen in front of you, instead of a book, may enable you to free your hands.)
- Practise, so that you know the story well; try to avoid sight-reading.
- Read meaning and not just words. (See above)
- Clearly distinguish voices (see below).

Voice and voices

Breathe

Project your voice, as you do when addressing your class, so that those at the back of the class can hear you without having to strain. Projection, however, is different from shouting; one can project while whispering, or hold back on projection while shouting. Projection, and the extent to which you project, is often about intention rather than, necessarily, about volume. Though, in some cases, to project better, you may simply need to raise your voice.

When nervous, one of the first things that often happens is we forget to breathe; people often find themselves running out of breath when presenting or storytelling. This is because breathing can become constricted to the upper chest as the stomach ties itself up in knots.

One of the easiest ways around this problem is to concentrate on breathing deeply from your belly – not only will it support your voice, it will also calm you down. Remember: when you get nervous, if you have prepared your story well, rehearsed and written your keyword list (see page 35), then the only thing to do before starting your story is to breathe in deeply and begin with your well-rehearsed opening line.

Whose voice?

There is another sense in which we use the word 'voice', it can also mean *who is saying what's being said*. It should always be clear to an audience *who* is saying the words that issue from the storyteller's mouth. The standard way to do this is to report who is about to speak or who has just spoken by saying 'and then she said: "I'm always here." or '"I'm always here," she said.' This method works very well, especially if the 'he saids' and 'she saids' are skimmed over as if they are not there, and treated more like a comma. Incidentally, as a storyteller you should avoid the use of adverbs after the 'he / she saids' – for instance 'he replied angrily' – because you have the advantage of being able to reply *in an angry way* rendering such descriptions superfluous.

Alternatively, and especially once you are more experienced, you can begin to drop the 'saids' on occasion. But if you do so then you need to find another way to indicate who the speaker is. This can be done with physicalisation or with the adoption of an affected voice or accent, and / or the use of props. For instance, as one of my colleagues once did, if you have explained that a character spends all her time sitting on a chair hating everything, then by sitting down in the chair that you – as narrator – indicated towards, this shows that you are now inhabiting the character and it may not be necessary to say, 'and then she said' – you may simply begin her speech. You must be careful when employing these kinds of more subtle devices. They have the benefit of making your audience work a little harder because they have to work out for themselves that there has been a shift from narrator to character but such ambiguities can also lead to confusion, so always have the 'saids' ready-and-waiting. Slipping one in later can help indicate, or confirm, to the audience who is speaking while retaining the benefit of keeping the audience on their toes. So,

As narrator: 'Miss Anthropy hated everything and she would spend her time sitting in her rocking chair [indicating the chair with hand] watching the TV hating everything she saw.' [Adopting a withered, screwed-up physical appearance while sitting in the chair and using an affected bitter sounding voice] *As Miss Anthropy:* '"I hate it when I see adverts, soap operas and documentaries," said Miss Anthropy, "I also hate..."' Etc. (Thanks to Philosophy Foundation Specialist Andy West for this example).

If the storyteller does not clearly delineate his move from narrator to character with careful use of voices, physicalisation and so forth you can see how easily the sense of the narrative could be lost to an audience, especially a young one.

Volume and projection

Subscribing to the Goldilocks Principle (see page 23) your default voice should be moderately loud so that listeners do not have to strain to hear you but so that you are not shouting as this makes for an unpleasant listening experience for the audience and will unnecessarily tire your voice.

Volume is helpful for emphasising a situation within the story. For example, if the characters in the story need to be quiet in order to avoid being eaten by a giant then you may turn your narrator's voice down to a whisper, heightening the need for quiet (within the story) and drawing your listeners in all the more. Of course, if your listeners are having to strain to hear you most of the time they will soon lose interest in your story, but there are times when making them strain to hear will help to draw your audience in. It's all about choosing your time and timing your choice well. A similar example comes in the traditional story of *The Timid Hare* (see Robert Fisher's *Stories For Thinking*, 1996) where a loud bang is central to the story. Shouting 'BANG!' unexpectedly when one occurs can help young children understand what has frightened the hare. Careful though! I over did it the first time I tried this and made someone cry (they were very young), an event which goes to show the effectiveness of the technique...

Clarity

It is of paramount importance that you make your words, phrases, sentences and thoughts absolutely clear. Clarity of expression comes only with clarity of thought so always know what it is you are trying to say. When you are unclear in yourself your words will be correspondingly unclear. (See Visualisation on page 48 for more on helping to prepare for clarity.)

Pace and pause

Again, your default voice should be neither too fast nor too slow. Find a good, moderate rhythm to pace your storytelling. Speaking too fast causes words and thoughts to trip over each other. An audience needs time for the images and scenes from a story to form in their imagination, if you speak too quickly you won't allow this to happen and they will become lost and consequently lose interest. If you speak too slowly the story will sound laboured and seem boring. That said, the correct use of *pause* is a very powerful tool available to the storyteller. Here are some suggestions for when pauses could be useful. There will be others but you'll need to be sensitive to when those times could be.

Take stock

Sometimes a pause is necessary for you to think about what's coming or to take a glance at your keyword list. If you do this then make sure that you do so at an appropriate place in the story. Finish the thought, scene or action before pausing; it won't seem so unnatural then and the audience will be less likely to know that you're unsure – it will seem that you are pausing for effect while you take the time to recollect. Steven Hoggins, a colleague of mine, was once preparing his class for an assembly and found that they had a tendency to look down into the piece of paper with text on and race through it. His advice was to read a sentence and then to look up at the audience to deliver it. This helped them to both address the audience and to slow them down considerably, improving the pace of their performance.

Transition

Pausing between events, characters' dialogue, scenes and so on can help to draw your audience in; when you pause, the audience will lean in towards you, physically demonstrating their desire to know what happens next. When speaking, and particularly when addressing an audience, many people have a tendency to fill space with words. The worry is 'if I'm not speaking or conveying something they'll get bored or lose interest'. The truth is the opposite of this. Spaces between words, thoughts and events help to foster expectation and anticipation. This is often the best way to get your audience wanting to know what's going to happen. (Thanks to Philosophy Foundation specialist Andrew Day for this insight.)

Audience anticipation

A well-timed pause can usher your audience along when you hope that they will anticipate something of your story before the situation is explicitly stated *in* the story, such as the second episode with the Roc in the Sindbad stories where it should dawn on the audience, as it dawns on Sindbad, that the ship had arrived on the island of the Roc and that the crew members had probably secured their own demise by breaking open the egg (see page 200). A pause is as good as saying, 'So, where do you think they are, then, and what do you think is going to happen?' No, it's better. A pause and a look is often all you need to elicit the (very satisfying) gasps from your audience that tell you *they've anticipated*. This facilitates your audience's understanding of the story.

Learning stories

When learning a story to tell, one question you must answer is whether you will learn the story word-for-word or not. Ruth Sawyer (1942) reports how the storyteller Marie Shedlock learnt her stories word-for-word but Sawyer suggests that, though her performances were excellent, this is more a dramatic performance than storytelling. Storytelling is usually understood to be an oral tradition and, as such, storytellers are not usually encouraged to recite. However, someone who does recite a story, poem or song will have many of the same issues a storyteller contends with, such as achieving a sense of *nowness* (see page 26), use of body language and gestures, and it must be remembered that these are all forms of storytelling in the broader sense. Interestingly, there is debate among scholars as to whether the storytellers of *The Odyssey* in ancient Greek times would have memorised the epic word-for-word or whether they would have improvised around a structure, inserting familiar stock phrases and sentences. It has been suggested that an *aoidos* was distinguished from the later *rhapsode*, in ancient Greece, by not being limited by reciting an already written text.

When attempting to achieve fresh talk (see page 28) and *nowness* I suggest that making your own telling around a general structure is preferable to a word-for-word recitation, and once you achieve fluency with this approach, it is the best way to lift a story from the page. Unless you have a very good memory for lines, such as my wife, for the rest of us recitation can be very time consuming.

Word and phrase-ticks

When working towards fresh talk there is the ever-present danger of ticks. The most common is, of course, 'erm...' or 'errr...'. Children, when storytelling, often insert 'and then...' between just about every sentence, as they try to think of what comes next (see *The Matches* session plan on page 99 to help them with this). We all have ticks in normal speech too: 'basically', 'literally', 'actually', 'like' and 'do-you-know-what-I-mean?' are some very common examples. Mine, perhaps not so interestingly, is 'interestingly'. These will spoil your storytelling, and, arguably, they are not great for your normal speech either. Sometimes a listener will become so aware of them that he or she will start to involuntarily listen out for the next use of a tick, which can become a distraction from whatever it is you are attempting to convey. At first, this may require something of a Herculean effort to resist, like trying to eat a sugar-coated doughnut without licking your lips! But it will become easier and eventually naturalised. This is very helpful if you are a public speaker; and your speech in general may well benefit from this effort.

Story-memorising and memorising stories

Take a brief look at the following list of ten randomly selected words then close the book and try to write them down, in order, on a piece of paper (no cheating!):

house	round
blue	Christmas
girl	loud
fish	chair
dice	bag

Most people can remember the first few words and the last few words but struggle with the middle ones. This is known as the *recency / primacy effect*. Many people also find recalling more than seven bits of information in their short-term memory difficult to do. The first thing to bear in mind when using memory techniques to help learn stories is that *story* itself is a memory technique. Stories are a very effective way of transferring more than seven units of information into the long-term memory. Look at another list of ten randomly-chosen words but this time read the 'story' that follows making sure that you fully visualise the scenes in your mind's eye:

frame	eyes
bear	bird
tea	heart
yellow	carriage
flower	shave

*Once upon a time there was a picture **frame** and within it was a picture of a terrifying **bear** but in the picture the bear was drinking **tea**, which wasn't so terrifying. Then along came a **yellow flower** and peering out from between the petals were two **eyes**. A passing **bird** swooped down to feed from the flower only to fall in love with the flower with all her **heart**. They got married and went off together in a beautiful **carriage** and while they travelled together they both had a **shave**.*

Close the book and recall the story's events and characters visually in your mind's eye, writing down the key words (above in **bold**) as you go. You should find it much easier even if you don't quite get it all right. The reason for this is that you have transformed the words into a sequential narrative structure with vivid images, all of which help to recall bits of information and in sequential order. Remember: the sillier and the more humorous (shave!), the easier you will probably find it to recall.

Keyword lists

When learning stories all one has to do is to reverse this process, so, rather than using a story to recall a list of words, use a list of words to recall a story. In both cases visualisation (see page 48) is essential.

Whenever you want to learn a new story, first of all read it through carefully out loud. By 'out loud' I mean either literally out loud or *as if* reading out loud. The point is not to skim over words or phrases but to allow each image to fully form in your mind's eye and to allow all the words to sound out. If your lips move while reading, this is a good sign that you are reading in the right way. Once you have done this you should read it again but this time create a *keyword list*. For each major event in the story try to find just one word – or at the most a short phrase – to help you recall that part of the story.

I have provided an example keyword list for the story *The Patience of Trees* (see page 118) and *The Promise-Slippers* (see page 123). However, I have deliberately omitted to do so for many of the other stories as that would discourage the reader from doing his or her own. Taking the time to create your own keyword list is vital if you are to properly process the story you are trying to learn. The fact of having done so will probably mean that you will not need to refer to it during your telling. However, the keyword lists will still be valuable later when you want to tell the story again, having not told it for a while. A quick read through of your keyword list is probably all you'll need to recall the story once more. It does however repay to read through the fuller version from time to time to remind you of some of the finer details of the story. It is also interesting at this point to see if, or how much, your version has digressed from or embellished the original.

Chunking

If you were to look at the following list of zeros and ones for ten seconds and then try to recall them you would probably find it difficult to do.

0 1 1 0 1 0 1 0 1 0 0 1 0 1 1

However, if you were to look at this list (below) you are likely to find it much easier even though both lists are the same arrangement of zeros and ones.

0 1 1 0 / 1 0 1 0 / 1 0 0 / 1 0 1 / 1

The reason for this is a phenomenon known as *chunking*. By dividing the numbers up in this way you will have turned fifteen bits of information into just five bits of information. Fifteen is well above what the short-term memory can hold but five is below. Many of us use this technique when we memorise phone numbers, for instance (though with the increasing use of mobile phones we learn phone numbers less often than we used to).

Three – the magic story number

A similar technique is used in storytelling to approach the learning of stories.

Remember: a story can usually be broken down into threes (example: the long story, *Sindbad and The Valley of The Diamonds* on page 186):

1 How Sindbad arrives at the valley of the diamonds.
2 What happens in the valley of the diamonds.
3 How he escapes the valley of the diamonds.

And each part can be broken down into a further group of threes.

1 How Sindbad arrives at the valley of the diamonds:
   1 Accidentally marooned.
   2 Finds the roc egg.
   3 Transported to the valley of the diamonds.
2 What happens in the valley of the diamonds:
   1 Realises he is rich but trapped.
   2 Encounters the snake in the tree.
   3 Builds the cage.
3 How he escapes the valley of the diamonds:
   1 Sees the carcass.
   2 Hatches a plan.
   3 Saved by men.

And, of course, if you need to, you can break it down into further groups of three, though it would probably not be necessary to do so. Instead of a long, linear narrative that lies dauntingly ahead of you, you will have broken the story up into much more manageable, bite-sized chunks. If you prefer, when making your keyword list you could use the 'in threes' method shown above.

Some people, annoyingly, will read a story once and have the whole thing pretty much ready to go. If, like the rest of us, you need a little more preparation, then use whichever of these techniques affords you the best results. With practice I can almost guarantee that your ability to memorise stories will improve.

Story sequences

Much can and has been said about the difference between narrative and story that is as unhelpful as it is helpful. I shall not go into this in any great detail here, but, relevant to the aims and objectives of this book, it can be said that, for example, the stories of Sindbad are part of the grand narrative that is *The Arabian Nights*; stories are often understood to have a beginning, a middle and an end, whereas narratives are continuous and open ended.

Stories are also sequential. This is thought by some to be a central aspect of story; one event should lead naturally on to another. There are a number of reasons for this. A narrative may not necessarily be presented sequentially; a story, however, is. When you 'story' a narrative one of the things you do to it is that you put the events of the narrative into sequential order. This property of stories will serve the storyteller very well when it comes to memorising a story or navigating a way through one. It should also be noted that this is particularly useful for storytellers who do not learn visually. A great deal is made of visualisation in storytelling but not all of us are primarily visual learners. If not, then the sequential*ness* of stories will play a vital role in your ability to learn them.

An abiding rule to bear in mind is that *everything happens in a story for a reason*. If anything is inexplicable or extraneous in a story, then it shouldn't be there. All features of a story, all the content, should tell the audience something; it should convey some kind of information. Notice that this is in contrast to reality, which has glitches. People say things that have no bearing on any significant events but stories do not behave like this. Stories have been shaped by necessity to include only the significant events, thereby signposting for the audience meaning and plot. It's as though the irrelevant material has simply been shaved off. When the storyteller says 'There was once a man and in his garden there grew a tree,' this tells you that the man and the tree are significant: they will both play a role in the unfolding of this tale. There will, of course, be other things in his garden but they will have been ignored by the storyteller because they have no role to play in the story.

Character desire and motivation

Just as sequence helps to tell a story so too do the desires and motivations of the characters. Characters in stories are simplified versions of real people, containing only a small set of desires and motivations. The king wants to marry the queen, the prince wants to kill the king, the captain wants to return his men home and the witch wants to capture the captain and his men. When someone is thirsty she wants to drink, when hungry, she wants food.

Odysseus is proud and consequently he desires to do things that otherwise would not make sense in a story. He stands at the front of his ship and, when he is at a safe distance, he taunts the cyclops Polyphemus, endangering his entire crew. Only his pride allows an audience to understand why he does this. So, other than recalling objects and events in a story one must also make sure that, through good storytelling, the audience has a firm understanding of just why each character does what they do. Make sure you, as the storyteller, know what each character wants and what their character is disposed to do. An earlier promise will make a character do things at a later stage that would otherwise be inexplicable. In stories as in life, character desire and motivation makes the inexplicable explicable.

Tone and register

The tone and register of your voice when telling stories is very important just as it is when trying to lull a baby to sleep or when praising – or telling off – your class. A monotone is not going to be very engaging and a consistently high register will sound shrill and off-putting.

Find a comfortable, mid-range voice to use as your default storytelling voice. This will change when you adopt character voices or when varying your tone for gathering pace in the story as exciting episodes unfold. But if your default voice – the one you use for the majority of the time – is overly affected your voice will quickly tire and the audience will find the storytelling laboured and unnatural.

Tone and meaning

It is amazing what you can do with the tone of your voice. A common strategy for showing the importance of punctuation is to take a sentence such as this famous example, 'eats shoots and leaves,' and then show how a comma can drastically change the meaning: 'eats, shoots and leaves.' (Truss, 2009) Think about that for a minute. But, of course, there is no punctuation – in this sense anyway – when storytelling.

Invisible punctuation

A less well-known example shows that *meaning* can be changed without the addition or subtraction of any written punctuation:

> 'We should not speak ill of our friends.'
>
> (Copi and Cohen, 2008)

Notice how the meaning of the sentence changes considerably if you put a stress on a different word. '*We* should not speak ill of our friends,' means that it may be okay for someone other than us to speak ill of our friends; or 'We should not *speak* ill of our friends,' implies that it may be okay to *think* or *write* ill of our friends. Carry on in this manner stressing a different word in the sentence each time and try to say how the meaning changes. (I have written a poem-version of this called 'Invisible punctuation' that can be found in *Thoughtings: Problems, Puzzles and Paradoxes in Poetry to Think With* by Peter Worley and Andrew Day, 2012.)

See 'Gestures' on page 43 for examples of physical punctuation.

Matching the register: adapting for different audiences

I often used to use a series of little stories / thought-experiments about time and time travel from Martin Cohen's *101 Philosophy Problems* (1999), but I found that I could only use them with older children (age 11 and up) because Cohen's language and register were clearly chosen for teenagers and young adults. One day, however, I wanted to use one of the stories with a Year 4 (age eight to nine) class because the issue it addresses had emerged naturally from a class discussion. I didn't have the book with me but having read it with other classes on a regular basis I had it memorised, so I *told it* and found that I was adapting the story almost unconsciously to meet the register of my nine-year-old audience. I also noticed that this audience was laughing much more than the classes I had read it to before. Not because Cohen isn't funny but because his tone of humour was somewhat over the heads of my primary school audiences. Through telling the story I was able to bring the humour to the level of my audience naturally. I realised that this insight would unlock a huge number of resources for a much greater number of age groups.

Conversely, if I were to turn up to a Year 6 class with a copy of *Knuffle Bunny* by Mo Willems (2005) under my arm they would feel patronised and annoyed that we were going to work with 'a baby's book'. However, if I were to simply *tell* the story I would be almost assured that they would respond appropriately. Given that the picture book *Knuffle Bunny* is such a rich resource for exploring the nature of language and meaning (unlocked so easily with the question: 'Is Trixie talking?') it would be a shame for a Year 6 class to miss out on what the book can offer just because it is seen as a baby's book. Storytelling is a simple way to side-step this particular barrier to the use of certain resources for thinking with stories.

Extension activity: exercises in style

See Matt Madden's *99 Ways to Tell a Story: Exercises in Style* (2006) for some very creative inspiration about how to adapt a narrative for different audiences, itself inspired by Raymond Queneau's book, also called *Exercises in Style* (2008). These books should also provide some inspiration for you to devise your own extension activities to get your class writing their own story in a variety of styles. For example, set your class the task of writing a story in the following formats (and / or others):

- a report
- a list
- a mind-map
- a storyboard (pictures)
- different perspectives (see 'the Rashomon effect' on page 27)
- a story.

Then ask them to analyse what it is they think makes each form what it is, and what distinguishes it from other forms.

Eyes, eye-telling and eye contact

Your eyes will be a very useful and important tool for your storytelling; *where* you look and *how* you look will enable you to tell a great deal while enabling your audience to understand a good deal from what you tell them. Wide eyes and an earnest look tells your audience that *this really matters*, or it can say, 'Can you believe it?' Closing your eyes can communicate the oceans of despair a character may be feeling. Breneman and Breneman (1983) recommend simply changing the angle of your look to indicate different speakers.

When I tell the story *Once Upon an If* (see page 85) I use books as props, and when I reach the part where Zadie opens The Story Book only to find empty pages, I flick through the book and try to communicate to the audience that it is empty, only with my eyes. When I hear some of them whisper loudly, 'It's empty!' I then say, 'The book seemed to be completely empty (flicking through the pages some more)... except for one page!' A change in my eyes and facial expression a moment before I say this last clause tells them, before I say it, that I'm about to challenge the absoluteness of the first clause ('completely empty') in light of the character gaining more information. All this can be achieved in a second when I use my eyes to supplement any other storytelling devices I may be using.

Unless you are specifically doing so for a storytelling reason, you should keep eye contact with your audience as often as possible. There is a problem however: there are many eyes in an audience and you only have two. Try to share your eye contact with different parts of the audience as regularly as you can. If there are those sitting so that they are in your peripheral vision only, make sure you attend to them explicitly with your eye contact from time to time so that they know you are telling to them as well as everyone else.

Movement, gestures and expression

Less is more

When I began telling stories I moved around rather a lot. It may have had something to do with the fact that I was often telling stories to very young children. And although silly and overstated movements can be very effective with younger children, it does tend towards *slapstick* and is not usually my preferred way to tell stories these days. Of course, it will depend on many things, such as the story, the age of the audience, and it is, to some extent, a choice of personal style; but, in my view, the best tellers use the 'less is more' principle. Here are some more hints to help develop this aspect of your story-telling. Breneman and Breneman's book *Once Upon a Time: A Storytelling Handbook* (1983) was particularly useful for this section.

One-spot storytelling

This is where you describe movement without moving from where you stand. If you want to physicalise walking, running, swimming or flying and so on then it is best to do so – especially if space is limited – where you stand. There may be times when you want to step out from your spot, for instance, if you want to make it clear that you are now representing or adopting the position of another character. Using the less-is-more approach an entire story can be told very effectively from just one spot.

Working in large spaces

However, when working with large groups and / or in large spaces there is a danger that those not proximate to the teller will become disengaged just like 'the children at the back of the class'. For this reason it is of the utmost importance to make those at the farthest reaches of the room feel included and spoken to. Under these circumstances it is allowable for you to move around the room, making use of the space as you tell the story. It will not be necessary to do this all the time but, from time to time, you may want to make a brief tour around the space, moving slowly as you tell, allowing you to make contact with the entire group. When doing this you must ensure that your voice is clear and well-projected, so that those who you may have your back to at any one time can still clearly hear you. You may decide to wait for an appropriate moment in the story to leave your spot at the front, such as when a character explores somewhere. Never have your back to an audience member for a second longer than necessary!

Gestures

If a character is climbing a rope, about to fire an arrow, or some other action that is easily represented, then do so with a minimal gesture. This can usually be done with no more than your hands and arms, though sometimes it will require a full-body stance, such as when repelling a monster with a spear!

Contradiction

In films it became standard for the music score to tell the audience information that the action does not. For instance, the action may tell of domestic bliss but the music may presage something sinister, contradicting the pictorial message. This contrasted with an earlier tendency in film scores to be straight-forwardly graphic, paralleling the action and movement as it was seen by the audience. As a storyteller you do not have the benefit of a score to contradict the actions and events of a story but you do have gestures, movement, tone and facial expressions. A character is asked by another off-stage character if he has the magic ring; you say 'he replied by telling her that he didn't have it' but while saying this you take a ring off your finger and hurriedly put it in your back pocket. If the audience has already been informed by the preceding narrative that he does in fact have the ring then this gesture is all that's needed to tell the audience that though he says he doesn't have the ring, really he does and that he doesn't want them to know.

In the famous scene when Odysseus is rewarded by the Cyclops Polyphemus, when he says, 'I like you, Nobody, and because I like you I shall give you a gift in return for the gift [of wine] you gave me: I shall eat you last!' I have Odysseus reply, 'That's very thoughtful of you, Polyphemus.' A great deal of humour is achieved – as well as discomfort – if, while you say Odysseus' words here, you use tone and facial expression to tell a different story to that of the words spoken: namely, that it's *not* very thoughtful!

Substituting

This is where a word is replaced with an action or gesture. This is a particularly useful device when working with young children, as it provides a signal to the children to say the word (especially if it is a repetitive word), phrase or chorus. Substitution can be very useful with other age groups too. For instance, an action or gesture can be used instead of a description or adverb. So, instead of saying '...he said while pointing,' you could simply point while delivering the character's dialogue. Or, instead of saying '...he said angrily', simply say what he said, *angrily*.

Anticipation

A particularly effective further element that can be added to your gestures repertoire is to perform the gesture *just before* you say the action the gesture is meant to represent. This anticipates features of the story and helps pull the audience along through the story, encouraging them to employ their imagination to piece the story together for themselves before you tell it. (See also audience anticipation in 'Pace and pause' on page 32.)

Physicalisation

Sometimes it can be helpful for your telling to physicalise a character in the story. This is not to everyone's taste and is not usually necessary; most stories can be told perfectly well without the need for this. However, adopting the physical characteristics, personality traits or idiosyncrasies of a particular character can help to more fully engage your audience (particularly younger audiences) by either aiding their visualisations or helping them access the story or follow it. Very often it will do all of these. If you use physicalisation then there are two ways that you can approach it:

Slight physicalisation

This is where, for example, you stay where you are (see 'One-spot storytelling' on page 42) and indicate with a slight change who you are. Perhaps nothing more than a slight bend in your knees and a squint tells your audience that you are now the grandfather character, possibly augmented with a slightly croaky voice (see 'Voice and voices' on page 29).

Full physicalisation

When you feel more confident you may decide to make much greater use of the space (see 'Working in large spaces' on page 42) available to you. For example, if telling Anthony Browne's *Little Beauty* (2009) then you may decide to physicalise the gorilla in the story by moving around the space as if you were the gorilla in its room, moving as a gorilla might. If you are using the cardboard box prop (see 'Minimal prop principle' on page 47), then you may have put the box in the centre of the room and have just said, 'they decided to give the gorilla a present which they left in his room one morning...' at which point you 'become' the gorilla who has just woken up. Maybe you scratch your head and move around the space before even noticing the box. Then, when you do, you move cautiously towards it, unsure exactly what it is. When you finally do go up close and open it, perhaps you recoil fearfully at first before finding the courage or curiosity to look in again. Your 'gorilla' facial expression changes from fearful to wonder as you peer in.

Having made a storytelling decision and having decided not to tell the children what is in the box your facial expressions and physicalisation both introduce the children to the character in a more immediate and visceral way and, in part, tell the story. Next, switching roles to 'narrator', you say, 'the Zoo scientists wonder what the gorilla will do with the defenceless kitten' and, as you say, 'the gorilla reached in and took out the kitten' you show, without having to say, exactly how the gorilla does so: namely, gently and with great care.

Audience participation in physicalisation

Sometimes, and again this will often be the case with younger audiences, you may want to involve the children kinesthetically with the story. Returning to the Miss Anthropy example (see page 30), when my colleague introduced his class to the character of Miss Anthropy, who, if you recall, hates everything, he explained how 'her face is all screwed up with hate like a fist' and then he showed them by tightly clenching his fist. Next, he asked the audience to have a go, 'how would your face be if it was like a clenched fist?' Of course, the whole class is then engaged in trying to achieve this with their faces.

Other times the children, if engaged with a story, will participate, unprompted. For instance, if I tell of a character running away from something and if I begin to (on-the-spot) run, the children invariably join in. If they do this, let them, and then indicate with your hands to stop when you are ready to continue. Otherwise, as I have found, they will continue, all the way off the cliff!

Using 'story space'

If the storyteller describes a dragon flying overhead then they can describe the dragon while looking up towards an imagined sky, adopting the point of view (and the space) of the character who sees the dragon. Alternatively, they could spread out their arms to *become* the dragon itself, looking down from the sky on the ant-like people below. The storyteller can be wherever she wants. And, what's more, she can change her perspective at will.

I remember seeing a colleague of mine, Rachel Kershaw, tell a story about a discussion between a native American grandfather and his grandson in a teepee. (The story was 'The Wolves Inside' taken from *Telling Tales* by Taffy Thomas and Steve Killick, 2007). She chose to sit next to the imagined teepee. She set the scene and then physically opened the imagined teepee to invite us (the audience) in to listen to their conversation. Her creative use of how the narrator inhabits the physical space within the story was extremely evocative and helped to draw us all into her story-world even though the story takes less than five minutes to tell.

Structure and the withholding of information (or The Odysseus Principle)

A story has two component parts: content and form. The same story told by two tellers may well have the same content but often it is the style and structure that really marks the difference between two tellings of the same story. Much of the 'Sheherazad's handbook' section of this book is dedicated to those elements that inform stylistic differences: how much pace, movement or gesture you will use to make a story your own. But much of my interest lies in how I piece the story together. Watch Quentin Tarantino's *Pulp Fiction* (1994), Harold Pinter's *Betrayal* (1978) or Christopher Nolan's *Memento* (2000) to see how chronological structure can be employed as an important part of one's storytelling approach. And, as we see with a film like *Memento*, it is not just a choice about how the information is shared but also about the experience the audience has and the reason for the audience-members experiencing it in that way.

Neither Tarantino nor Pinter were the first to play with story structure in a novel way. Take *The Odyssey*. It begins towards the end of the narrative and with Telemachus, Odysseus' son. The section that is usually thought to begin the narrative, the abduction of Helen and the war between the Greeks and the Trojans, is not officially part of the narrative and only gets a brief mention in passing by the characters Demodocus and Odysseus. The best known sequence of adventures that includes the episodes with the Cyclops, Circe and the Underworld (among others) is told about half way through the book by Odysseus when he recounts his adventures to Alcinous and his retinue. (Surprisingly little detail is given to this sequence.) Given that the order of Homer's story is not the same as the order of the narrative (this, by the way, helps to see clearly what the difference between these two terms is) I have always taken it as licence to all subsequent storytellers to play with story structure even though they may feel that they should remain faithful to the content.

Playing with structure is an important resource for the storyteller but it can also be an excellent tool for helping encourage thinking from your audience. (See 'When to ask a question' on page 63 in Chapter three: Storythinking).

Minimal prop principle

Given that this book is aimed at teachers first and foremost, and given that I am not an expert in the use of props, I will not dwell on extraneous features to the storyteller's craft such as costumes, props and the use of musical instruments. Professional storytellers make good use of all of the above but I shall introduce a few basic ways that props can be used for your storytelling without requiring anything too outlandish.

I have often found that props are unnecessary but from time to time have included their use in a minimal way. My first use of a prop was when telling the story of 'Gyges' ring' (that can be found in *The If Machine*) in which a shepherd finds a magical ring of invisibility. When describing the ring – and the shepherd putting it on and taking it off – I found myself, without thinking, doing the actions with my wedding ring. I noticed that the children's eyes had become transfixed on the ring as I manipulated it as if they were wondering whether my ring was really magical. I have also seen storytellers do similar things with artefacts from a museum's collection, for example, weaving a story around the artefact.

Minimal prop advice is to find something that can act as a focal point around which the story and the storytelling can then revolve, something for the audience to focus their eyes on but that otherwise does not interfere with your normal storytelling procedures. It has the benefit of helping to keep them engaged and focused and gives their eyes something to look at other than you. If your story focuses around a crown (see *The Magic Crown* on page 169) then you may use a toy, wooden or card crown as your prop, or if a book (see the story *Once Upon an If* on page 85), take an appropriate looking book with you for your telling. However, it is worth remembering that you can tell most stories very effectively without any props.

You can also use a nondescript item and transform it as the story progresses. When telling the story of *Little Beauty* (see my comments on page 45) I use a cardboard box as a prop. When the gorilla is given a kitten I use the box to act as the container in which the kitten is presented to the gorilla. The box later becomes the television that the gorilla and Beauty watch when the gorilla becomes angry and that he goes on to smash up.

Visualisation (or how to follow a recipe)

Nothing beats experience for recalling information. If you have made a journey then giving directions for that journey is often relatively easy to do. If you have cooked a recipe, and especially if you have done so more than once, then writing it down for someone else is reasonably straight forward. However, if you have only looked at a map or if *you* are the one receiving the directions, it is much harder to retain the information. How many times have you reached a certain part of a recipe only to discover something time-consuming that you had missed when reading through, such as marinating overnight?

Stories trigger a part of the brain that corresponds with the actual act, so if children are hearing you tell of an exciting ride on a bicycle it activates a part of the brain activated when they are actually riding a bike. This is because a story, as opposed to a recipe, naturally produces *visualisation* in its audience. Visualisation is more than simply understanding a chunk of information: it is the act of *seeing* something in your mind's eye in a way that resembles *really* seeing something. This can be illustrated well enough with a recipe, of all things.

Pick up a recipe book and open it up at a randomly selected page. Now read the recipe through once in the normal way. Then read it again, but this time, fully engage the imaginative part of your brain. You may even want to use your hands to help with this, acting out the various parts of the recipe as you go. If it says 'finely chop an onion and then fry gently for a few minutes or until the onion has changed colour', do this in your mind using your hands to stir the onion while holding the pan as you complete the task. Carry on through the recipe in this way and you should notice how much easier it is to recall the recipe and how much better you understand what the recipe requires.

Telling a story a good number of times is like being on a journey or cooking a recipe. You can also use visualisation techniques in preparation for telling a story that you've not told before, in much the same way as the exercise above with the recipe. To do this you need to imagine that you are in front of a class and then you need to tell the story out loud or 'out loud in your head' (see Keyword lists on page 35). In other words, you need to go through each word that you will say, responding with fully formed pictures and images of the events of the story in your imagination. You should only need to do this once before facing your audience but if you are less experienced do it as many times as you can: while waiting for a bus, walking to the shops or driving to work. Better still, find someone to tell it to such as a partner, your children or some willing friends.

How to describe a story

Here's a quick visualisation exercise: I want you to imagine that you are a camera in a film. Sometimes you'll go closer to show the audience a detail, such as the decoration on a vase. Other times you'll pull back to reveal a panorama such as the view from a ship. Sometimes you'll simply focus on a dialogue between two characters, but other times you'll spend lingering over the details of the environment in which the scene is set.

Storytelling is the same only you don't have a camera, you've got to produce a similar effect equipped only with your voice, your body and your words. You're not just the camera operator, you are also the director so it's up to you when you 'zoom in' and when you 'pan out'. Paying heed to 'The Goldilocks

Principle' (see page 23), too much over-elaborate description may begin by enchanting your listeners but they will soon lose interest unless there is a plot to carry them along. But just giving them a list of the events in an '…and then… and then… and then…' way won't capture their attention in the first place. You will have to make *your own decisions* about when to do what. One very good test for whether you're getting it right is the reaction you get from your audience.

Here are some hints and exercises to help you:

- Watch films and see what the camera does and ask yourself – from the point-of-view of the storytelling – why the decision was made to make the camera do this or that. (Remember: everything happens for a reason.)
- Read stories and see what 'the camera' does in them, imagining the story is being filmed.
- When telling a story use description to set the scene but give yourself the following rule: *don't take too long; keep things moving.*
- Watch 'the camera of the heart!' Sometimes it will be necessary to imagine a camera filming how people are feeling, or thinking. The same principle applies: sometimes 'pan back': ('Kalypso wondered what Odysseus was thinking but could not see in his face') and other times 'zoom in': ('upon hearing the screams of the men Odysseus was hit hard by an intense feeling of regret at what he had done').

Vocabulary

Unlike the reader of a written story, the storyteller is not committed to any one range or level of vocabulary. The vocabulary the storyteller chooses to employ will depend on the audience she finds herself in front of.

As a basic rule of thumb *choose simpler words for younger audiences.* However, there's more to say on this. Children like to be challenged and they like to learn new words so don't be afraid to use longer or unfamiliar words. Here are some suggestions for how to introduce less familiar words. And remember: *context is everything.*

- One way is to put in a longer word and then to repeat the meaning immediately afterwards: 'The storm eventually *subsided* (which means *it slowly went away*) and then…' A more subtle version of this is to follow the unfamiliar word with a *clue-word* to help the children infer its meaning: 'The storm eventually *subsided* until it was *calm* again'. The clue-word here is 'calm'; if subsiding results in being calm then it is relatively easy to understand the role a word such as 'subside' is playing here. This is different from understanding what a word means and, although short of being a full understanding, it enables a listener to continue to access a story without interrupting the flow even though it contains unfamiliar words. In fact, this is the way most of us have learned many of the words we know. It is also why we often have slightly inaccurate definitions of some words.

- Meaning can also be helped along with hand gestures or movement. This technique also helps to maintain the flow of the story. So, for instance, when you say the phrase, 'The storm eventually subsided', as you say the word 'subsided' you could raise your hands to approximately face-height with your palms facing down and then bring your hands down to just below your neck indicating a gradual downward movement. This, combined with the aforementioned clue-word technique, can really help to convey meaning.

- Another technique is to ask if anyone knows the word so that they can explain it to the class: 'The three of them gathered together to *confer* with each other about what to do. Does anyone here know what 'confer' means?' This shouldn't be done too often as it interferes with the flow of the storytelling, but is good if there is an important or crucial word, or one that reappears in the story, that it is important the children understand. With very young children it is effective to have at least one 'interesting' (new) word in each story, such as Beatrix Potter's use of the word 'soporific' in *The Tale of The Flopsy Bunnies* (1909). She uses the technique of providing a clue-phrase of *feeling sleepy* after its introduction:

> 'It is said that the effect of eating too much lettuce is "soporific". *I* have never felt sleepy after eating lettuce; but then *I* am not a rabbit.'

- And finally, if no one knows the word, you could ask them what they *think* it means. Always repeat the full context (the necessary phrase, sentence or stanza) to help them with this. I often find that even the youngest children can infer an approximate meaning of some surprisingly advanced words simply from the context. You can always clarify or provide a more accurate definition once they have had a go if you feel it is necessary. This should seldom be done as it takes rather a lot of time, but it can be a particularly useful strategy when using poetry with a class. (See the 'Unfamiliar words' exercise on page 166 for an exercise with poetry that makes use of this strategy.)

Developing your instant thesaurus

Here's an exercise to help develop your powers of description using your vocabulary. Read the following through.

*The **knight went** up the **winding** stairs **silently** and **eventually** came to a **door**. He listened but **heard** nothing, so, he **carefully** tried the door. Upon his first* *touch it unlatched itself and **swung** open as if to **invite** him through. **Beyond** the door **was darkness**.*

Now read it again and stop on a highlighted word such as 'door' and now try to think of three different ways to say or describe this word: 'portal', 'entrance', 'escape'. Notice that you could think of a word that simply acts as a synonym or you could think of a more evocative word that is more context-dependent (in this case 'escape') – get creative! Then, carry on reading until you come to another highlighted word and repeat the same exercise. Don't limit this exercise to only the highlighted words; also try to replace a word with a phrase (e.g. 'eventually' = 'after some time'). This exercise is best done with paper, writing down your three words. Think about which words work best and why. This will depend very much on your audience.

When and what to describe

It is important to choose carefully when to describe and when not to (see 'The Goldilocks Principle' on page 23). It is important to remember the following rule: do not over-describe. The three main reasons for describing are: 1) to build an atmosphere, 2) to help imagine a scene and 3) to provide information or draw attention to something. Take the following bare bones of a story from Plato:

- An earthquake reveals a long-lost city to a lone shepherd.
- One of his sheep is lost in the city and he needs to retrieve it or he will have to pay for it from his wages.
- He goes into the city in search of his lost sheep.
- There he discovers a throne with the remains of a dead king sitting upon it.
- The shepherd removes a ring from the finger of the skeleton king.
- Another earthquake covers the city once more and the shepherd narrowly escapes.
- Once he is safely on the surface again he discovers that the ring has the power to turn him invisible.
- With this power he turns the queen against her husband, kills him and takes his place as king.

Take a look and try to identify where description would be apt and also note where it would not, then read on.

The following aspects would be augmented by a little extra description:

- The dead king (builds atmosphere).
- His narrow escape (creates tension).
- His discovery of the power of invisibility (this is the focal point of the story).

I would suggest not spending too much time describing the following:

- The city (it has no role to play other than providing the story with the ring).
- The earthquake (its only role is to open the earth to provide the ring through a strange but plausible event).

The smell of old books – engaging the senses

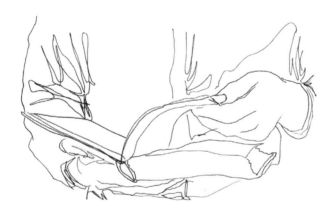

As a storyteller you find many ways to draw your audience in. Many little things come together to create a big effect: the earnest look in your eye, the pauses between sentences, phrases or sections, the lowering of your voice are all examples of little things that add up to a larger, overall effect. One of those 'little things' is the occasional and well-timed appeal to the senses.

I tell a story about three friends who decide to bake a cake, in order to engender a discussion with young children about fairness and justice. At some point they (the characters *and* the audience) have to decide how the cake should be cut and how much of the cake each child should get (see my book *The Philosophy Shop*, 2012, page 235). To help me draw them into the story so that they feel something of the investment of the characters, I take them through the whole process, describing how one of the characters saves all her money and how another goes to the shops to buy the ingredients. (I ask the children to tell me what sort of things they will need to buy.) Then, as I describe the children waiting for the cake to bake I say that 'they all sit looking at the oven' and how '20 minutes seems to take forever' and that 'they can all smell the warm aroma of a baking cake wafting towards their noses'.

As I'm telling them this some of the children smile, others lick their lips while others inhale slowly through their noses, some of them close their eyes. The appeal the storytelling has made to the senses has triggered something Pavlovian. Just as the smell of frying garlic has the power to trigger salivation in preparation for eating and digestion, so too can storytelling trigger similar physiological responses with nothing other than the power of the imagination.

This example is a full-on assault of the senses but there is another, more subtle, way to make use of sense-activation with an occasional peppering to add a sense-dimension to the listener's created world. When I tell the story of *The Little Old Shop of Curiosities* (see *The If Machine*, page 111) I might include something like the following:

The audience has been asked to imagine a strange and out-of-place shop squeezed in among a row of familiar shops near where they live. As they investigate further, they push open the door and just before they close it again to leave I might say,

> 'Just as you are closing the door you catch the smell of old books – a smell you happen to love. You decide to push the door open again and to take a proper look inside…'

Of course, this results in their going in and discovering something quite amazing (see the story to find out what!). In this telling, the discovery entirely hinges on the accidental – and apparently insignificant – detail of a chance aroma. And activating their sense of smell has also helped to realise the scene in the mind's eye – or is it the mind's nose? – of the listeners. Even those who may never have smelled old books (an increasing possibility as we move further into the digital age) are prompted to imagine what old books may smell like. If this is the case, then their imaginations have been properly and actively engaged.

Picture books and how to tell them

As in the example of *Little Beauty* (see page 45), picture books can make excellent resources for finding tales to tell, but be careful when choosing. Some of them work very well and transfer very easily to storytelling but others transfer less well. One reason for this is that some picture books are more than just stories with pictures, sometimes the storytelling is shared between both the text and the pictures so that only a partial amount of the information on any page comes from the text alone. A good example of this is *UFO Diary* (2007) by Satoshi Kitamura. This does not necessarily mean that it can't be told; for instance, if the picture *contradicts* what the text says then this contradiction may be conveyed perfectly well through good storytelling (see 'Contradiction' page 43).

Reading picture books can also call upon your storytelling skills. (See exercise using *Not Now, Bernard* on page 29).

For a list of picture books complete with Task Questions for use with classes log on to the online resources that accompany this book. A regularly updated list is available from The Philosophy Foundation website: http://www.philosophy-foundation.org/resources/picture-books.

3

Storythinking

Enquiry

An essential part of using stories for thinking is that you must have a method or procedure for conducting a discussion. You may already have one but, if not, here is a quick procedural guide. For a more detailed account of how to conduct a philosophical enquiry (also known as PhiE) see *The If Machine*, page 1–45.

1 *Talking circle*: Sit your class in a circle or horseshoe shape. Eye contact is very important if you want successful discussion-based sessions.
2 *Tell your story*: See 'Sheherazad's handbook' for suggestions of how to do this effectively.

The enquiry section

3 Stop the story at the appropriate time, as indicated in the chapters, to run the discussion part of the session. The enquiry part of this procedure is contained within this box.
4 (Optional or alternative) *First Thoughts*: If using this part of the procedure skip step five and go straight to six for their First Thoughts then run the enquiry with no task questions.
5 *Task question (TQ)*: Do any necessary set-up, then ask the TQ, writing it up clearly on the board.
6 *Talk Time*: Allow two minutes or so where the children speak to each other in pairs or small groups. Take this opportunity to find out what some individual pairs think.
7 *Gain their attention*: After a couple of minutes of Talk Time use a visual signal explained at the outset to get the class's attention. I simply put my hand in the air holding the ball that I use for speaker management.
8 *Begin the enquiry*: Remind them of the TQ and begin the enquiry.
9 *Facilitate the enquiry*: Allow as many of the children as possible to speak without insisting, and use the basic strategy of 'anchoring and opening

---

up' or 'if-ing, anchoring and opening up' (see page 74) to facilitate the discussion. But remember not to say what *you* think! Your job is to facilitate a dialogic discussion between the children – one that is built naturally and step-by-step from comments and responses made by the children, leading toward a discussion that is structured, sequential, disciplined and rigorous.

10 *New Task Questions*: If a new TQ emerges from the discussion, or you want to move to a further TQ from the book, then set the new TQ and repeat the process from step three.

11 *Continue, or finish, the story*: If necessary, leave enough time to continue with what's left of the story before moving on to another enquiry in the story or ending the session.

First Thoughts

Sometimes, before or instead of asking a TQ you may simply want to let the children respond to each other with their First Thoughts about the story. If so, skip step five and go straight to six for their First Thoughts. If a discussion emerges from this then run your enquiry around it. If a question emerges then write it up as a TQ. Alternatively, if nothing fruitful comes of First Thoughts then go to step five and set a prepared TQ in the usual way. Sometimes First Thoughts is used explicitly to undergo a necessary comprehension task before any enquiry can begin. (See 'Emergent Questions and Enquiries' on page 59.)

Talk Time

Whenever a question is put to the class, always allow some Talk Time – 'two minutes' for the children to talk to each other about the question either in pairs or small groups. The number of people talking in each group is not so important. The only rule is that *everyone should be talking to at least one other person*. Note that this is a good time to find out what the quiet children think as not everyone is initially comfortable sharing their ideas with the whole class. Make especial use of the 'Imaginary disagreer' strategy (see page 74) with pairs or groups in Talk Time.

Questions

Below are details of the types of questions that are used in this book.

Task Questions

Example (from *The Patience of Trees* on page 118):
Task Question: Who, if anyone, is free in this story?

Task questions (TQ) should be asked explicitly, and written up on the board, so that the class can follow the session plans. They are carefully selected to bring the class to the intended area of focus and to help the class see a particular controversy. They are tried-and-tested in the classroom so if you want to maintain the focus and controversy outlined in the chapter, it is important to make sure that these questions are asked *exactly as written*; any small change to the question can change the nature of the discussion significantly, so only change a TQ if you explicitly wish to alter the question in a specific way to suit your own teaching ends. Sometimes there will be more than one TQ. I have placed them where it would be suitable to discuss the issue the TQ highlights. However, you may well not want to discuss all the TQs in any one story in the same session. (See 'Finding the right question' on page 59 for hints when devising your own TQs, also see 'Using Task Questions' in Appendix 1 on page 209 for quick view steps.)

Nested Questions

These follow the TQ and provide a sequenced list of questions that are, in some important ways, related to the TQ. They pave the way for possible discussion routes. Example (also from *The Patience of Trees*):

Nested Questions:
- What is freedom?
- What is free will?
- What makes someone or something free?
- The leaf believes that it is free. Is it?
- The river believes that it is free. Is it?
- At the end the learning tree believes that it is free. Is it?

In contrast to the TQ, Nested Questions are the implicit questions that lie behind a discussion. Take a look at the list of Nested Questions and notice how they relate to the TQ above. Having a list of Nested Questions is important for you to be prepared for the enquiry.

Emergent Questions and Enquiries

Emergent Questions are the questions that emerge during a discussion that are not listed, and an Emergent Enquiry is a discussion that arises in response to a story though no TQ has been asked. Sometimes all that is needed is for the story to be read or told and for the class to be given an opportunity to respond. See 'First Thoughts' on page 57 for how to allow this to happen during your enquiry procedure. Emergent Enquiries are also an important part of the Concept Box approach too (see 'The Concept Box' on page 77). For quick view steps of the Emergent Enquiry procedure see Appendix 1 on page 209.

Finding the right question

A good question for enquiry is one that, when you ask it to a class or group, elicits lots of yeses and noes. This tells you that the controversy behind the question has already bitten. However, if they do not see the controversy straight away, it does not mean that there isn't one. See, for example, the Imaginary disagreer strategy on page 74 for encouraging a class to explore a question so that they may start to identify a controversy not at first seen.

I am always on the lookout for new stories that I can use to get children thinking around an issue; stories that bring out controversies. Once a story has been found that brings a thinking issue out really well the next problem is finding the right question to engage the children with the issue so that they recognise the issue or controversy without my having to outline it. I have included questions, both Task and Nested (see above), throughout the stories of this book so that you don't have to find questions for yourself. However, you may still, for whatever reason, want to find your own TQs for the stories so here are a few things to bear in mind (these are general guidelines, so they may not always be the case):

A good Task Question...

- is *concrete* – it is an 'in the story'-question (see below) (Good: *When he is in the valley of the diamonds is Sindbad rich?* Avoid: *What is it to be rich?* – this is a Nested Question.) Of course, an enquiry should move towards abstract questions but should not begin abstract.
- uses *simple language* even though the question may be profound or complex (Good: *Is it fair?* Avoid: *Is this situation an example of justice?*)

- *does not introduce new concept-words* not already present in the story; questions that introduce related concept-words that are not mentioned in the story are Nested Questions.
- is, if possible, *not conditional* – that is, of the form 'if… then…?' (Good: *Is it fair?* Avoid: *If we assume that x, y and z then, under these circumstances, would it be fair?*) Sometimes conditional questions are necessary, and much of your questioning during an enquiry will need to be conditional (see If-fing, anchoring and opening up on page 74), but, on the whole, the TQ itself will benefit from being non-conditional.
- is *closed* (Good: *Is it magic?* Avoid: *What do you think magic is?*) Closed questions keep responses focused; as long as you remember to 'open up' children's responses (see page 75) this should not hinder an enquiry's progress. (See also my article 'The Question X' in *Creative Teaching and Learning*, 2013. Available online from The Philosophy Foundation website, see page xxi.)

Emergent Questions as Task Questions

Many of the best questions I use have come from the children themselves. In *The Luckiest Man in the World* (see page 177 and online) I could not think of a good question for the story but during a discussion around the story with some eight and nine-year-olds one of the children asked the following question: 'What's going to happen next?' I then asked him what he thought would happen and what it would mean. He said, 'I want to know if it's going to be lucky or unlucky'. With the evidence of the wonderful discussion that followed from this I felt that this was the question I had been looking for: *When Polycrates' ring had been returned to him in the belly of the fish was it lucky or unlucky?* So, even if you've not yet found a good question don't be afraid to tell the story to your class so that you can allow the children to help you find one. And like the ring in the belly of the fish it should find its way to you. (Also see 'The Concept Box' on page 77, by the end of which procedure many good questions should have made their way to the surface; questions you will be able to use with other groups.)

Socratic Questions

With any story or stimulus there is almost always a general concept-question that can be asked of the form 'What is X?' ('What is luck?' in *The Luckiest Man in the World* on page 177, 'What is freedom?' in *The Patience of Trees* on page 118, 'What is a promise?' in *The Promise-Slippers* on page 123). These are usually known as *Socratic Questions* and are so called because of the central role these questions played in the philosopher Socrates' questioning method. I have, where appropriate, included Socratic Questions in the list of Nested Questions. I think that they are a little too general and abstract to begin a discussion and it is for this reason that I have selected more concrete TQs for beginning an enquiry; however, most TQs aim towards these Socratic Questions. The Concept Box procedure (see page 77) is designed to get the children identifying these sorts of concepts for themselves. (See 'Concrete and abstract' on page 65.)

Creating stories around questions

At other times you may have a question but no story. In this case a story must be written to fit around the question to give it a context. If you can write stories, it is much easier to write something new than it is to find a story that perfectly fits your question. If you don't write stories then now is your chance to change that.

Try the following story-writing exercise. Here is a question that came from an 11-year-old girl called Clarissa: *Where is the edge of a cloud?* The issue I have identified in this question is that of *vagueness* given that it is far from clear how one would decide exactly where the edge of a cloud is. (To prepare, find out more about the issues surrounding the notion of vagueness by consulting *The Stanford Encyclopaedia of Philosophy*: http://plato.stanford.edu/entries/vagueness/). Now write a very short story, no more than a paragraph or two in which to place this question. Once you have completed the task take a look at my own attempt below (an original short story in the style of a parable, complete with Task and Nested Questions ready for use with your class). Compare yours with mine. Try them both with classes and see how they go down. Make a note of what works and what does not from each one.

As Clear As the Edge of a Cloud

A long time ago in Japan, Chen, a Buddhist student, had been studying to reach enlightenment, which is a Buddhist word for 'understanding' – something Buddhists try to reach through meditation. He had been trying to reach enlightenment for many years now, yet he still didn't feel that he had come anywhere near finding it. So, he travelled a great distance to see a renowned Buddhist teacher and he asked him, 'O Wise One, where will I find enlightenment?' The teacher replied, 'You will find enlightenment where you find the edge of a cloud'.

'Thank you, O Wise One, thank you, thank you,' said Chen, more than grateful. He was so pleased to finally have an answer to his question. He stepped outside and looked up and said to himself, 'I have finally found the way to enlightenment, all I have to do now is find the edge of a cloud.'

Task Question 1: Where is the edge of a cloud?
(There are two distinct enquiries here, so try to answer Task Question 1 before attempting to answer Task Question 2.)

Nested Questions:
- What is a cloud made of?
- How would you find the edge?
- How would you know when you have found the edge of a cloud?
- When a cloud of steam comes out of a kettle where is the edge of the cloud of steam? (IMPORTANT: be very careful around steam from a kettle!)
- Does a cloud have an edge?
- When a cloud rains where does the cloud end and the rain begin?
- Is water the same thing as a cloud?

Extension discussion idea

Task Question 2: What do you think the Buddhist teacher meant by the answer he gave to Chen?

Nested Questions:
- What has the edge of a cloud got to do with enlightenment, or understanding?
- What is enlightenment? What does it mean?
- Why did the wise man give the answer he did?
- Is the answer he gave clear or vague?
- Does it mean anything?

When to ask a question

Traditionally, stories are read to children through to the end so that the children witness a problem and then a problem being solved. There is often a 'moral' at the end of the story that acts as a lesson to its audience. You can see this most clearly in stories such as *Aesop's Fables*, many of which have the moral spelled out at the end of the story, for example, 'It is best to prepare for the days of necessity' (*The Ant and The Grasshopper circa Fifth Century*) – clearly designed to 'correct certain tendencies [in children] by showing the consequences in the career of the hero' (Shedlock, 1915). As I have already said, although this approach with stories has its place, it is limited when the aim is to activate critical and creative thinking in the audience. When stories are used in this way the audience is engaged, but passively. In other words, they are in a receptive mode rather than a participatory one (see 'Making effective use of the moral' on page 64 and 'Stories and thinking' on page 14 for more on this).

Key to the use of stories for thinking is the active engagement of an audience through some kind of participation. But I don't mean physical audience participation in the usual sense. The point at which a question is asked in a story and a discussion held is of paramount importance in order to get your class thinking actively. Story-form often includes a *tension* or *crisis point*; the point at which a problem, dilemma, or difficulty is met by one of the central characters. Many will be familiar with 'The story mountain' image used to capture these structural features of many stories. (See Appendix 3: 'Story mountain and extension activities' on page 220)

The point of tension in the story is often, though not always, the best place to stop the story in order to engage your audience critically: when the tension has been created but before it has been resolved. The audience's motivation to think comes from the story at this point in a number of ways: there may be a problem that the children recognise as a problem and therefore the human instinct, once a problem is recognised, is to try to solve it. They may also be motivated to solve the problem for a character or to help move the story on, for instance, if a problem needs to be solved in order to find out what happens next. (See 'Narrative problems' on page 67 for more on this.)

A friend of mine told me how a good history teacher, who once taught her as part of the French Baccalaureate, used to stop the lesson at a crisis point in the historical narrative. For instance, before explaining what a particular military leader such as Wellington actually did in a given situation he would ask the class, 'If you were Wellington what would you do under these circum-stances?' Only once the class had explored their ideas based on the historical information they had would the teacher go on to say what did *in fact* happen and what choices were made. In my friend's view this engaged the students' critical faculties much more deeply than had they been told beforehand what Wellington had done.

Making effective use of the moral

Once your audience is in the active mode of critical and creative engagement you will find that the children are more likely to respond to the moral of the story critically. However, very often a question is needed to spark a response. In a wonderful picture book that I use with very young children called *The Saddest King* by Christopher Wormell (2008), a moral is said by the boy character at the end of the book. He says 'You have to be the way you feel'. This is said because the king had made happiness compulsory in his kingdom but had subsequently come to see the error of his ways. Because the children had already been engaged in an enquiry earlier during the session all I had to do was to say to them, 'Is the boy right, should you be how you feel?' It didn't take them long to start to find situations where, actually, it wouldn't be appropriate to 'be how you feel' such as situations that call for inner restraint. They went on to qualify the moral of the story. (See my comments at the end of 'Stories and thinking' on page 14.)

Books with shortcomings and errors

Thomas E. Wartenburg, in his book *Big Ideas For Little Kids* (2009), says that rather than avoid books that make obvious errors we should instead 'use the errors in the book to teach the children the need to think for themselves and not to accept something just because they find it written in a book'. Wartenburg makes very effective use of *The Important Book* by Margaret Brown (1949) despite his observation that it 'makes claims about the important thing about various entities that are quite apparently false. For example, it says that the important thing about an apple is that it is round'. Rather than explicitly teach the children to 'think for themselves' – which brings with it an uncomfortable irony – when I have run sessions using this book I have encouraged the children's critical engagement with one very simple question: 'Do you agree with the book?' One five-year-old said, 'Apples are not round, they have little bumps on them,' to which another of his classmates said, 'There's no such thing as a perfect circle'; something to which the philosopher Plato would have some sympathy. See my comments in 'Thinking with' and 'thinking about' on page 16.

Ask a question from the story

Sometimes the question will come directly from the story itself. Again, in *The Saddest King*, during an exchange between the boy and the king, the king asks the boy 'Why would anyone want to be sad?' This is an excellent question for thinking, and all the better for already being in the story; nothing extraneous is needed to engage the audience. It is a good idea to stop the story when you encounter a question like this. That way, the children get a chance to think for themselves before the thinking is done for them by the story. Of course, not all questions asked in stories are going to be as fruitful, but remain on the lookout for any good thinking-questions already formulated for your class within a story.

Concrete and abstract

When using stories and questions as the basis for discussions in your class it is often best to begin with a question that is rooted within the story. However, one should be ready to move to questions that abstract 'out of' the story later on. So, in *The Valley of The Diamonds* on page 186 you will notice that the question, 'When he is in the valley of the diamonds, is Sindbad rich?' is very much about the particular situation and characters in the story. However, more general and abstract questions to be ready to move to could be: 'What is it to be rich?', 'What makes something valuable?' and so on. This approach helps younger audiences ease their way into more abstract discussions. It also means that the story is being made use of. If you were to tell a story and move straight to a general question like 'What is freedom?' it means that, not only have you almost disrespectfully ignored the story you have just told, but you will also not be able to use the situation in the story to explore the ideas and apply the ideas the children have had. Remember: stories serve as hypothetical practice runs for similar real-life situations that children may find themselves faced with later in life (see 'Ethics through narrative' on page 12).

'In the story', 'Out of the story' and then 'Back in again'
Follow this model for how to question around a story (example from *The Promise-Slippers* on page 123):

> 1 'In the story' (concrete). 'Does Lira have a choice?'
> 2 'Out of the story' (abstract). 'What is a choice?'
> 3 'In the story again' (concrete). (If X is a choice) Does Lira have a choice?'

At point three the story is being used to test the theories and suggestions. If someone says that 'a choice is when you are completely free to decide to do something', then this should be tested against the situation in the story: 'So, does Lira have a choice?' The child may then decide to apply the definition, 'No, because she's not completely free,' or she may qualify her definition, 'Maybe you don't have to be completely free, just a little bit.' Not only does this help the children think, it makes good use of the story in order to do so.

Real-life analogies

Recall Charlotte's response to the boy in her class who said, 'What have monsters got to do with real life?' She said, 'It's not really about monsters, it's about choices.' Making analogies with real life situations can not only help the children make sense of a story, it also helps to have them see the relevance of the story and then apply their considerations to real-life situations. So, for example, if the story contains a dilemma, such as the Scylla and Charibdis dilemma from *The Odyssey*, you could introduce a dilemma using a more familiar situation to the children such as a boy who knows that his best friend stole from his teacher and who finds himself torn between loyalty to his teacher and to his friend (see 'Charlie's Choice' from *The Philosophy Shop*, 2012). Either you could think up an analogous situation for yourself, or, better still, invite the class to construct one. Alternatively, you could model for them with the first couple of examples, handing the task over to them subsequently.

Narrative enquiries

'The Ceebie Stories' in *The If Machine* began life as one story called *Jack's New Friend* that I wrote in response to a teacher who said that the class I was to be working with would be focusing on two themes as part of their curriculum: *friendship* and *robots*. *Jack's New Friend* looked at whether one can have a friendship with a robot, inviting the children to investigate the nature of friendship, relationships and personhood. But when I looked at the story more closely it struck me that there was so much more to think about, not least, the issues that spring from artificial intelligence – only touched upon in the story in order to set the story up. So, I set to work writing more stories to include the other themes in *Jack's New Friend*.

The first thing I noticed was the way the children related to and invested in the characters of both Jack and Ceebie and how this helped to engage the class more keenly with the discussions and enquiries. Each week they really wanted to know what would happen next in the Ceebie saga. This narrative thread was bringing the children to the philosophy in a more meaningful way, providing a powerful learning motivation. The success of the Ceebie stories gave me the confidence to tackle an even bigger narrative project: Homer's *Odyssey* (see *The If Odyssey* for the result).

Narrative problems

Many of the problems around which the enquiries are based in 'The Ceebie Stories' are not abstract philosophical problems for the children, but problems that emerge from the difficulties faced by the characters in the story. This means that part of the motivation to solve problems, and therefore engage with the enquiry, comes from the narrative; the children play a role in helping the characters in some way, or in moving the plot along. For instance, the first enquiry in 'The Ceebie Stories' is based around the question *what is a friend?* The children explore this question only to return to the narrative in order to apply the fruits of their enquiry to Jack's difficulty when his human friend, Tony, challenges him. Tony says that Ceebie can't be a real friend because he is only a robot made from plastic, metal and wires.

The second part of the enquiry for the children is based around the question: *is Ceebie a friend?* Using the model described above here are the three parts to the questioning employed around this enquiry:

1 'In the story' (concrete): *Is Tony right that Ceebie is not a real friend?*
2 'Out of the story' (abstract): *What is a friend?*
3 'In the story again' (concrete): *Is Ceebie a friend?*

On the next page is the concept map (see page 70) that was drawn during this enquiry.

When the class returns to the story at point three, check what was said at point two against the question 'Is Ceebie a friend?' So, 'Can Ceebie talk?' 'Can Ceebie play?' and so on. The concept map can be a very good way of drawing attention to tensions and controversies. For instance, at some point during this process the facilitator may ask the following: 'If a friend "helps you", then is Ceebie a friend?' Presumably, if Ceebie can help Jack (and in the story he does, with his homework) then the child may think that Ceebie is a friend. However, if, as someone else has said, a friend needs to be able to 'feel what you feel' (this may mean something like 'empathise') then it is far from clear that Ceebie satisfies this condition and, in fact, given the underlying controversy here (Is Ceebie alive?), this would be an excellent basis of an enquiry using the following question: *Can Ceebie feel what you feel?* (An implied nested question is: Can Ceebie feel at all?)

Child-centred questioning

Notice that the facilitator did not ask:

'If a friend is "someone that helps you" then is Ceebie a friend?'

instead they asked:

'If a friend "helps you" then is Ceebie a friend?'

The reason for this is because the evidence from the concept map (see above) suggests that the child did not say, '*someone* that helps you', they said, 'a friend helps you'. If the facilitator were to insert 'someone that' then they would have pre-empted a conceptual move; they would have introduced an assumption: that a friend must be 'someone' rather than 'something'. Because this move was not made by the child, it would subtly *lead* the discussion which would therefore become less child-centred.

The general principle to follow here to help with this (rather subtle) technique is: [The conceptual movement principle] *only use what the children give and then provide the conditions to allow them to move the discussion forward rather than moving it on yourself.* For instance, in this example, a child may say – in answer to the question 'If a friend "helps you", then can Ceebie be a friend?' – 'A friend can be anything as long as it helps you, so I think Ceebie can be a friend.' But then someone else may say, 'A friend can't be anything; it can't be a wall or a flowerpot'. The facilitator could then, quite legitimately, ask 'If a friend cannot be a wall or a flowerpot, can Ceebie be a friend?' (This question would be an example of *iffing* and *anchoring* back to the question – see page 74). The group is now contesting, for itself, this aspect of the enquiry rather than having been lead to the controversy, artificially, by the facilitator.

If this challenge had not come from the group at this point, then it would have been an appropriate time for the facilitator to invite the group to make

the challenge. She could do this by saying, 'So, can a friend be anything? What about these: a) A person? b) A teddy? c) A pet? d) A book?' Following the advice of 'the conceptual movement principle' (above), it is always preferable to see if you can find a way to allow the group to make these conceptual moves for itself before doing so yourself.

The Thinking Kit

This section has been written to include the core *teaching thinking strategies* used and developed over the course of the books in the *If* series, *The If Machine* and *The If Odyssey*. I have tried to provide an exposition of each of the strategies as succinctly as possible so as not to take up too much space in this book while providing the reader with essential strategies. For more on teaching thinking strategies see, in particular, *The If Machine*, The Philosophy Foundation website (www.philosophy-foundation.org) and the bibliography section at the end of this book. Before reading below, and if you haven't already done so, take a quick look at 'Concepts' on page 18.

Concept map

The simplest example of this is writing a single word, for the concept under investigation, in the centre of the board, such as 'Fair', 'Beauty' or 'Love'. In order to unpack the concept and / or to explore the class's understanding of the concept you should write up all their attempts to say what they think the said concept is or means. An example of a concept map is as follows.

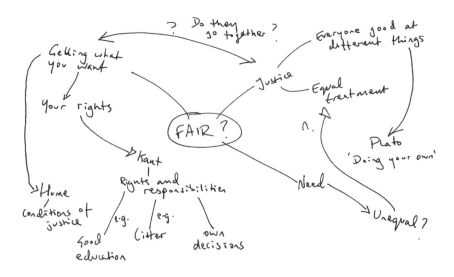

Key things to bear in mind are that you should use these only as an *aid* to discussions, so make sure that they don't become a barrier: don't worry too much about presentation and punctuation, for example. You can also write up full statements or questions in the centre of the board and then focus on the contained, relevant concepts, for example, 'Is the prisoner free?' where the relevant concepts would be 'prisoner' and 'free' (see 'Break the circle' below). Concept maps help to bring out tensions in a class's understanding of a single concept (see example in 'Narrative problems' on page 67). These tensions help to fuel discussions.

Carve it up: drawing distinctions

One of the most important tools in any philosopher's toolbox is the ability to identify and then draw distinctions. For example, the ability to notice when a concept such as *freedom* needs to be 'carved up' into further more subtle concepts such as *mental freedom* and *physical freedom*. For instance, in *The Patience of Trees* (see page 118) someone may suggest that the learning tree, at the end of the story, is mentally free even though it is not physically free as it remains rooted to the spot. Conversely, it may be suggested that the leaf is physically free but, not being the captain of where it ends up, is therefore not mentally free.

To encourage the children to draw distinctions in the classroom, all you have to do is notice when they may each be using a different meaning of a single word such as 'free' or 'good' or 'love'. Clues that this is being done are often indicated in the following kinds of comments: '*In a way* he is free and *in a way* he's not…' or 'It's half and half…' or 'Well, yes *and* no…' If they do not explicitly identify the distinctions themselves, then you can ask the following question: 'Do you think there are different meanings of the word 'free' in this discussion?' If they say 'Yes' then ask them: 'What do you think they are?' For older children there is no reason why you cannot explicitly tell them what a distinction is and how the technique works. This is a very good habit for them to get into and once you have introduced this technique to them they will probably start to draw distinctions themselves, unprompted.

Break the circle

'Break the circle' is based on the Socratic Question (see 'Socratic Questions' on page 60) and can be employed to circumvent a classic obstacle to using Socratic Questions in enquiries. The obstacle is that children have a habit of engaging in circular thinking. For example, if you ask children what *growth* is, they will often reply with, 'it's when something grows.' Here is a game / activity to help break the circular-thinking habit.

Choose a word from the list below and ask the children to tell you what the word means, but then say that there is a catch: 'You mustn't use the word in your answer'. Write up, on the top left-hand side of the board: 'It is…' to help them stick to this stipulation, then give them some Talk Time (see 'Talk Time' on page 57) in pairs. After a minute or two ask them to share their answers with the class, concept-mapping (see above) as you go.

- think
- love
- mind
- grow
- try
- do
- number

Once the children have been introduced to the game you can use the technique at any time when a child provides a definition or explains a word or term or if you want to explore a concept more deeply.

Examples and counter examples

Good thinking is often equated with logic and rigour and sometimes the creative aspect of thinking is forgotten. One way in which thinking can be very creative is in the use of examples and counter examples – the latter being something children have a natural tendency towards: 'But what if…'

Examples

When children say things generally, or abstractly, encourage them to provide a real-life example to help make their point. If they can't think of one, you could enlist the class to think of an example on their behalf – this also cultivates a collaborative effort. Because of their illustrative qualities, examples make ideas more accessible to more people.

Child A: Sometimes it is okay to lie or steal.
Teacher: Can you think of an example when it would be okay to lie or steal?
Child A: Erm… not right now.
Teacher: Can anyone think of an example when it would okay to lie or steal?

Child B: If you are poor and starving hungry then if you have to lie or steal to feed your children then it would be okay?

Counter Examples: 'But what if...'

A counter example differs from an example in that it is where someone provides an example in order to refute a claim. Children tend to do this unprompted:

Child A: I don't think that it's right to lie or steal, ever.
Child B: But what if you were poor and you had to steal to feed your children?

Sometimes it can be helpful to actively engage them on this task, for instance, when they all agree with a claim and therefore leave it unchallenged (see 'Imaginary disagreer' on page 74):

Teacher: So, what does *fair* mean?
(So far, everyone has agreed that 'fair' means 'getting what you want'.)
Teacher: Can anyone think of an example where you get what you want but it is not fair?
Child A: If you *want* more than everyone else, that wouldn't be fair?
Teacher: So, what does fair mean? (To child A)
Child A: It's fair when everyone gets the same.

Counter examples and falsification

Counter examples are also very useful for falsifying general claims:

Child A: All birds fly.
Child B: A penguin is a bird but penguins don't fly, so not all birds fly.

In this case, because the claim made was general, that all birds fly, only a single example is needed to refute it; it is quite unnecessary to mention ostriches or kiwis for the refutation to be successful.

Imaginary disagreer

This is a teaching thinking strategy that can be used in all sorts of different ways that asks a child, or children, to imagine that there is someone who disagrees with them. This helps to encourage them actively to seek alternative points of view. If you have two children, for example, during Talk Time, both of whom agree with each other and have therefore ceased to think about the issue, simply ask them to imagine that *if there was someone in the room who disagreed with them, then what do they think he or she would say*. The next step is to ask them what *reasons* they think their imaginary disagreer would give. This can be used with pairs, groups and also with the whole class (see 'Split debate' page 76). Sometimes the children will change their own minds because of what their 'disagreer' said!

If it, anchor it, open it up

Like a Swiss army knife this is *three-strategies-in-one* and, like a Swiss army knife, it is a strategy to keep on you at all times. I will begin with anchoring:

Anchoring

This is a deceptively simple technique where the facilitator brings the child back to the case in point by re-asking the Task Question with a neutral tone. For example:

A)   (Task Question: 'Is the tree free?')
    Child: 'It can't move even though it wants to.'
    Facilitator: (anchoring) 'So, is the tree free?'
    Child: 'No.'

Anchoring helps to:
- Keep the discussion focused.
- Keep contributions relevant.
- Reveal hidden relevance.
- Link ideas to the Task Question.
- Avoid dismissive comments from the teacher.
- Avoid premature judgement on the part of the teacher.
- Avoid unnecessary confrontation.
- Prompt children to contribute.
- Formulate and express formal arguments.

Opening up

This is how one keeps the virtue of their questioning 'open' even if 'closed questions' are being used:

B) (Task Question: 'Is the tree free?')
    Child: 'It can't move even though it wants to.'
    Facilitator: (anchoring) 'So, is the tree free?'
    Child: 'No.'
    Facilitator: (opening up) 'Why?' (or 'Could you say more about that?' or 'What reason do you have for that?' etc.)
    Child: 'Because if you can't move you're not free…'

These strategies complement each other so that they form the basis of your question-asking in the classroom.

Opening up helps to:
- Keep discussions moving.
- Elicit more information from the speaker.
- Make use of closed-questioning techniques such as *if-ing* and *anchoring* without closing down the discussion.
- Encourage justifications from the children.
- Encourage the formulation and expression of supporting reasons (formal arguments).

Many of the Task Questions (TQ) that feature in or after the stories are in the form of closed questions. It will be taken as read that after each TQ the facilitator should always remember to 'open up' the question again. Each TQ, though not written as such, should be read something like this:

Task Question: Is the leaf free? *If so, why? If not, why not?* (Or whatever opening up expression is most suitable.)

If-ing

'If-ing' is a form of questioning that makes use of the conditional sentence structure ('if… then…') in order to engender hypothetical thinking. Here they all are together:

C) (Task question: 'Is the tree free?')
    Child: 'No, because it can't move.'

Facilitator: (iffing) 'So, if it could move, like the leaf, then (anchoring) would the tree be free?'

Child: 'No.'

Facilitator: (opening up) 'Why?'

Child: 'Because, even though the leaf moves, it's not free because it doesn't have a choice where it goes.'

Facilitator: 'So, do you need choice to be free?'

Child: Yes.

Facilitator: (opening up) 'Why?'

Child: Because…

If-ing helps to:
- Avoid factual obstacles to a discussion.
- Keep the discussion conceptual.
- Test ideas against the Task Question.
- Test different hypotheses.
- Consider alternative points of view (the *imaginary disagreer* is an example of *if-ing*).

Debates

Discussions that have a binary nature (e.g. X or Y, X or *not*-X) lend themselves well to debates. If you feel that the children need to get up out of their seats then try these debate methods for your enquiry:

Split debate

If you find your class unanimous on an issue thereby threatening to jeopardise your discussion, then try the following. If the dispute is between two characters in a story then each of the two sides could be asked to role-play each of the two characters:

1 Split the class in two.
2 Tell one half that they are to adopt position X.
3 The other half should adopt the other position in the debate: not-X or Y.
4 The two class halves then spend a minute or two putting together some reasons in support of their position.
5 Then they have a dialogue across the room with each other, taking it in turns to have one speaker from each side make a contribution, role-playing if necessary (see above).
6 Half way through, you could get them to swap positions and spend some time arguing the other side of the case.

7 At the end of the debate each member of the group should make their own decision having heard all the reasons from both sides of the argument. They could each share their decision and their deciding reason at the end.

The walk across debate

1 Mark a line, using a metre ruler or something similar, about a quarter of the way across the room; do the same at the other end of the room.

2 Invite those that think X to stand at one end of the room behind the marker and those that think Y (or *not*-X) to stand at the other end of the room behind the other marker. Once in place they should sit down on the floor.

3 There should be a place in the middle of the room, between the two ends, where those who are undecided or who think something other than X or Y, X or not-X, should be able to take their places.

4 Allow children from different parts of the room to speak, taking turns as in the above method (Split debate). Speakers should stand up.

5 Once a couple of people have spoken, allow a few seconds for children to change places if they want to. It is often a good idea to ask children who have changed places to say *why they changed places*. Reasons that motivate a change in position are often good or interesting reasons and are likely to contribute to a good dialogue. It also discourages children to move just to be with their friends if they think they will be asked to justify their move.

The Concept Box

The Concept Box is a general technique for helping children develop their own discussions around central concepts (*fairness, love, punishment* etc.) without the need for task questions. It broadens out and then focuses in, as described in the following diagram:

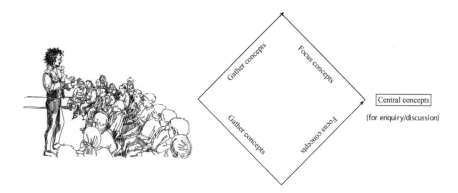

Isolating concepts in various ways is standard practice in many approaches to doing philosophy with children. The first part (the broadening-out part) of this procedure is called *concept fishing* (a term coined by Grace Robinson of Thinking Space who shared this part of the process with me and from which I developed the full procedure of the Concept Box). The second part (the focusing-in part) I call *concept funnelling* and it encourages the children to identify central concepts.

I find this a particularly useful way of approaching poetry and stories but it can be just as fruitful with all kinds of other stimuli. (All examples are taken from doing the Concept Box exercise following the poem *The Square That Didn't Fit In* on page 172 with some Year 5 children, age nine to ten).

The Concept Box

1 Begin by reading the story or poem.

Comprehension stage

2 After some Talk Time in pairs, allow the children to say whatever they like in response to the story or poem. Encourage them to ask questions or to put to the group any words or phrases (or anything, for that matter) they don't understand. This is a general comprehension aspect to the process so don't worry too much about them getting off-track. Always invite the group to answer any questions; avoid doing so yourself. (Examples of questions asked during the comprehension stage: 'Why did the monster go to Circle-Land?', 'Why didn't circles fit in his mouth?', 'I think the square didn't fit in because he wanted to be a circle on the inside even though he looked like a square on the outside.', 'What does malicious mean?')

Concept fishing

3 Next, set the class the task of trying to say *what the story or poem is about* to their talking partner but then stipulate that they must try to reduce this to just *one word* (you could allow hyphenated words). Say that you want as many of these 'key words' as possible but that there must be no repetition (Facilitator: 'If someone says your word either put your hand down or think of another one'.). Encourage everyone to take part. Again, don't worry if they miss the point or choose inappropriate words, as steps four and five will help to re-focus the discussion. (Examples of keywords following *concept fishing*: 'confused', 'mysterious', 'strange', 'shapes', 'crazy', 'weird', 'alive', 'lonely', 'unsure', 'misunderstanding', 'hungry', 'death', 'squircle'.)

Concept funnelling

4 Once they have completed step three ask them to look at all the words that have been gathered and to choose the one word they think *best captures what the whole poem or story is about* – the word that 'really gets to the heart' of the story or poem. I often ask for someone to give an example to the class of

a word they think *won't* be on the final list (in this case someone said 'hungry' and then, when asked why, he said, 'because that only happens in one bit'). I then ask someone to give an example of the kind of word they *do* think will be on the final list (in this case someone said, 'misunderstanding' and when asked why: 'because the square is misunderstood by the other squares and the monster misunderstands the square when he said he's a circle...'). Ask them to be ready with a reason why they chose the word they did. Limit this exercise to a set number of concept-words, such as five, so that they are encouraged to choose the more central ones. (You could make this longer if you feel that they have not quite got there yet, but only have as many words as necessary). Once this is done, rub off, delete or separate the other words. (Example central concepts by the end of *concept funnelling*: 'shapes', 'unsure', 'confused', 'misunderstanding', 'squircle'.)

Exploring central concepts
5 Next, have them debate these inclusions and / or say why they think (i.e. *justify / explain*) the story or poem is about the chosen concept-words or not. (Examples of questions and contributions from both the facilitator and the children: 'Are *confused* and *unsure* the same?', 'Can you be unsure without being confused?', 'It's about misunderstanding')
6 Now, use these concept-words to focus the discussion by asking the children to – as well as *justify* and *explain* – *compare, connect, clarify, challenge, analyse* and / or *revise* the concept-words in the context of the story or poem. This makes the discussion both general / abstract (Facilitator: 'What is it to be *unsure*?') and concrete / particular (Facilitator: 'What in the story makes it about *misunderstanding*?'). Used carefully and with considered questioning from the facilitator during the steps one to six you should be able to generate an enquiry without the need for a task question or for a process of question formulation and selection.

Optional Emergent Question
If a suitable question for enquiry emerges from this process, then it should not be ignored; this could be the question that the enquiry is then based around. In the example of *The Square That Didn't Fit In* one Emergent Question was 'Was the square a *squircle*?' This included the Nested Questions: What is a squircle? Can a square also be a circle? (Not only was the question emergent, but so too was the word 'squircle', invented by nine-year-old Élody as part of the *concept fishing* part of the process). See 'The Concept Box' on page 210 in Appendix 1 for quick view steps.

Bite and sting: tense and person for thinking

In philosophy one of the central conceits of the school of philosophy known as existentialism is that dilemmas are experienced. They are

not thought about in the abstract or considered propositionally; when someone is faced with a dilemma it should *bite*; and decisions *sting*. You will notice the inescapable first-person*ness* of all this. In stories *tense* and *person* can be used to help make a problem *bite* with an audience. If you tell a story in the second person and in the present tense a listener can be affected by the *nowness* (see page 26) of a story, when presented in this way.

Give the audience a role in the story

When I tell *The Odyssey* there are certain stories where I tell the children at the outset that they will play the role of Odysseus' men. This enables you to make present to them some of the more intense sections of some of the stories. For instance, the claustrophobia of the sequence in the cave with the cyclops or the despair when their ships are lost and the crew are blown back out to sea in the story of Aeolus and the bag of winds are more keenly felt when under-taken by the class in role.

Re-toothing a dilemma

Sometimes dilemmas in discussions can remain *bite-less* in that the children can very easily find themselves 'in the middle' or 'on both sides' of the dilemma. One appropriate way to give a dilemma its teeth again is to ask them to role-play a character's point of view in their considerations. For instance, if they were Odysseus or Sindbad, then they would not be able to sit on the fence of an issue: as a captain, Odysseus has to make a decision *one way or the other* as to whether he tells the crew about the hidden monster Scylla; Sindbad has to make decisions because he is actually in the situations – it's not abstract for him. This is the nature – as the existentialists like to point out – of decisions and choices. Thinking with stories is a great way for a class to practise responding to a decision's bite.

Put your audience into the story

This is different from giving them a role because of another use of the second person perspective. As in the story *Flat Earth* (see page 143), when you give them a role they inhabit a character, they are not present in the story. You may well say 'You did this and you did that' but you are telling them – for example, in *Flat Earth* – what the time-travelling scientist is doing and seeing. However, in the story *The Magic Crown* (see page 169), the 'you' refers to the audience. The story tells of something that it is supposed has happened – or is happening – to each individual listener.

An exercise in second person thinking

To see the power of the second person when used in this way, particularly for getting audiences thinking, consider the following story. (As with all the examples in the book presented for the teacher, this can also be used with an appropriately-aged class for discussion.)

A man, let's call him Bob, has recently made a terrifying discovery. It turns out that Bob is not Bob at all but in fact another person called Fred. Here is what Bob has recently discovered: he was once Fred, an unpleasant man who was convicted of a terrible crime, but instead of being locked away he was given the option of having his memories wiped and replaced with new ones giving him a completely new identity. The new identity and memories are those of Bob. Bob is a nice person and would never do any of the things that Fred did. In fact Bob finds the thought of them quite repugnant. But one day, a victim of one of Fred's misdemeanours spots Bob (who of course looks just like Fred) at the supermarket and demands that justice be brought to him. Bob is arrested and put on trial. The question the jury have to answer is this: should Bob be punished and held responsible for the crimes committed by Fred?

Adapted from Julian Baggini's *The Pig That Wants To Be Eaten* (2010), itself adapted from the film *Total Recall* and itself adapted from Philip K. Dick's short story *We Will Remember It For You Wholesale*.

Consider how you would answer this question before reading on:

This time imagine that it's not Bob but YOU that has been put on trial. Everything that is true of Bob/Fred above is true of YOU. It is YOU that stands accused of the crimes committed by Fred. You have no memory of ever having committed these crimes but the facts suggest that you – as Fred – did indeed perform the alleged actions. Is it right that you be punished or held responsible for crimes you have no memory of ever having committed?

From my own observations, the tendency of most people who consider these questions in the third person is to think that Bob *is* responsible for the crimes committed by Fred because it was the same actual, physical person that did it – he's just changed his memory, and he did it to escape justice. But the moment the question is re-framed in the context of the second person, in other words, the moment it is *you* and not 'Bob' or 'Fred', people resist accepting responsibility: 'How can I be held responsible for something I don't remember doing, even if the same *physical* person did it? I'm a nice guy after all! Don't I deserve a second chance?' The interests and sympathies of the considerer have changed through the power of the second person perspective (see Strawson, 1966).

The power of this simple shift in the narrative perspective is quite striking and it shows just how making this shift in a story, or in how you address your audience, can motivate an audience to think in a very different way. (See the comments made by the little girl about whose side the audience are supposed to be on, in 'Point of view and sympathy' on page 26). Furthermore this difference in thinking is itself worthy of reflection and reconsideration: does this fact about how I've changed my view on this issue in any way make my view on who is responsible reliable or unreliable? This raises further questions about truth in stories and the reliability of narrators in stories (see 'the Rashomon effect' on page 27).

Part 2
A Treasury of Stories

Once Upon an If (part 1)

Starting age: nine years

Themes:
- The nature of story
- Tropes, devices and clichés
- Plot, structure and characters

This story lends itself to the use of props (see page 47). If you would like to tell this with props then you will need two books, a larger book for The Big Story Book (preferably decorative to meet with its description in the story) and a smaller one for The Little Story Book. I wrap the larger book before the class arrives so that I can open it at the appropriate time in the story; I also place the smaller book under a table or chair on the other side of the room from me, in advance, so that I can retrieve it (almost magically) when it appears in the story.

In this, and the next story, it is important to stop the stories at certain times, such as where I have indicated, in order to engage the children actively in the story. This is important to help them prepare for the creative writing part of the exercise. By asking the class to say what they think will happen, what might happen, or what should happen, they are not only thinking creatively about how the story will unfold, they are thinking within the narrative confines of what has already happened up until that point. This is important given the particular aims of the 'Once Upon an If' story-writing exercise on page 97. (See, in particular, the question in *Matilda, The Fireless Dragon* where the children are asked to say what they think the water monster should do – or believe – when faced with a dragon that may, or may not, be able to breathe fire.) Log on to the online resources that accompany this book for a PowerPoint supplement to this story. This will help the class to follow the story but also introduces the basic outline of the activity they will be asked to take part in after the stories have been read or told. I have included in the text instructions when to show each numbered slide. Do not show a slide until it says, in the text, to do so, although the title page [Slide 1] should be open at the beginning of the story. (See Appendix 1 'Quick view steps' *Once Upon an If (part one)* on page 207 and 'Storytelling procedure with slideshow' on page 212.)

The story

Zadie was a little girl who loved stories. Her mum travelled far and wide around the world for her work. While travelling in the Middle East she was sold a very special object by a street seller at a bazaar in Turkey. She took it home as a gift for Zadie.

On her birthday Zadie opened up the present that she was sure was a book from its shape and weight. She wasn't very excited at the prospect of a book for her birthday, but when she took off the wrapping she found something she really wasn't expecting. It was a book beautifully bound with leather and a cover decoration made from real silver, curling and winding all around the book's cover and spine. The silver also formed the words 'The Story Book'. Now she really was excited. 'Thank you Mum!' she said.

Her mother, however, had a puzzled look on her face. 'What is it?' Zadie asked her.

'Oh, it's just that, when I bought it from the bookseller in Turkey –'

'Turkey! You bought this in Turkey?' Zadie interjected.

'Yes, from Turkey,' said her mother. 'As I was saying: when I bought it from Turkey I was sure the title was in Turkish. Funny how your memory plays tricks on you,' she said, more to herself than to anyone else.

'It's beautiful!' said Zadie, and then she kissed her mother. To Zadie, Turkey was a far-off, exotic place that brought to her mind magic carpets and minarets.

Zadie became distracted by all the other presents that she had to open and with all the fun things she did on her birthday and so didn't get to open the book all day. She went to the zoo and then came home and had a party with all her friends.

That night, when she lay in bed, she remembered that she hadn't opened The Story Book yet. She reached down to the pile of presents she had collected throughout the day and pulled the book out from the bottom.

She became enchanted again by the beautiful cover and her eyes tried to follow the twisting and curling lines that decorated it. But she could never follow one line to the end. Eventually she opened it…

Flicking through the pages she was disappointed to see that it was empty. Or, almost empty, for there was something on the first page only. [Slide 2] There was some writing with a picture above it of a stick person standing in front of a crudely drawn book that lay on the ground in front of it. The writing underneath said, 'Hello, I am the character from this book. You will need to tell me who and what I am. To do this you will need to use the book that is in your room – not this one; the other one. Take a look!' There, the writing ended.

Zadie thought that this was a very strange book indeed because if this was all that was written then it wasn't a story at all. But then something caught her eye just over the top of the book. In her room, across from her, lay another book that hadn't been there before. 'Wow!' she said as she decided that The Story Book must be magic.

She put down the book and jumped off her bed to retrieve the other, smaller one. She opened it to the first page and found only the words [Slide 3] 'Who am I?' written at the top, the rest of the page was empty. She turned the page to find [Slide 4] 'What am I?' at the top of the second page and [Slide 5] 'Where am I?' at the top of the third page; [Slide 6] 'When am I?' at the top of the fourth page and [Slide 7] 'What if...?' and [Slide 8] 'Who else?' at the top of the fifth and sixth pages. She had no idea what they could mean. 'Oh no!' she said, 'Now I'll never find out who's in The Story Book!'

That night it took her ages to fall asleep, she just didn't know what to do with the books. And she was so disappointed to discover that they had nothing but mysteries in them.

> **Task Question 1:** What do you think the questions in the little book mean?
>
> Nested Questions:
> - What should Zadie do with the books?
> - Can the mystery be solved?
> - What would you do?

But the new day brought with it an idea.

The first thing she did was to see if both books were still there. They were. Then she took her favourite pen and opened the smaller book that had appeared, she could only imagine magically, the night before. She opened the book to the first page where it said 'Who am I?' and she removed the top of the pen and wrote, 'You are…' then she stopped and wondered what name she could give the character. She realised that she could give the character any name she wanted. [Slide 9] 'You are… Matilda,' she wrote. Her mum had told her that she and her dad had nearly named Zadie 'Matilda'. Then she wondered about what sort of a person Matilda might be.

> **Task Question 2:** What sort of person would someone called Matilda be?
>
> Nested Questions:
> - Would a Matilda have any particular characteristics at all?
> - Does a name have anything to do with what sort of a person you are?
> - Does someone called Matilda have to be a girl?
> - Do you think Zadie would have been a different person had she been named Matilda?
> - *TX* (see page 7) *name-change*: imagine that you have had your name changed. Perhaps you have travelled to live in a new country where your old name was too difficult to pronounce. Are there any names you could have that may affect your personality or what sort of person people think you are? What about:
>   - Hilary? (Both a boy's and a girl's name)
>   - Biff?
>   - Farquhar?
>   - Are there any other names you can think of that might significantly affect you or the way other people see you?

Under the question 'What am I?' at the top of the second page Zadie wrote, 'You are a girl.' [Slide 10]

Zadie closed the little book then ran back to her bed, climbed up and opened The Big Story Book.

Task Question 3: What do you think she will find?

This time, instead of the stick person there was a picture, simply drawn, of a young girl about the same age as Zadie and underneath the picture it said,

Once upon a time there was a girl and her name was Matilda. [Slide 11]

It was written in beautiful, middle eastern-style calligraphy. The picture also showed Matilda holding and reading the book that had been on the floor before.

But then it occurred to Zadie that Matilda didn't have to be a girl, and a sudden rush of freedom surged through her. She crossed out 'girl' and instead wrote the word 'dragon' into The Little Story Book [Slide 12] *so that the story in The Big Story Book now read* [Slide 13],

Once upon a time there was a dragon and its name was Matilda…

There was now a picture of a dragon reading the book instead of the girl that had been there before.

A shiver ran through Zadie's body as she realised what was happening. She thought about what she could do. She took in a deep breath and lifted her pen to begin her story…

> **Task Question 4:** So, what has happened?

...As she breathed out, her breathing out gave her an idea, so Zadie wrote these words down in her Little Story Book under the question 'What if...?' [Slide 14]:

What if there was a dragon that couldn't breathe fire?

She opened The Big Story Book and, starting with a title

Matilda, The Fireless Dragon

it read [Slide 15]:

Once upon a time there was a dragon called Matilda. Matilda was a dragon that couldn't breathe fire and she lived in a...

Zadie realised that she was going to have to think of somewhere a dragon would live. So she lifted her pen and, using The Little Story Book, told Matilda where she lived under the question 'Where am I?'. Very carefully, she wrote [Slide 16],

Matilda lives in a cave all by herself and she likes being alone.

When she opened The Big Story Book again it now read [Slide 17]:

Once upon a time there was a dragon called Matilda. Matilda was a dragon that couldn't breathe fire and she lived in a cave by herself. All she wanted was to be left alone.

'Oh!' said Zadie, 'It's sad.' Then she realised that she needed to tell the book what other characters there would be so that the story could be finished. [Slide 18] Under the question 'Who else?', she wrote:

There will be a grumpy princess, the princess's parents, the king and queen; an annoying knight and a monster made of water...

Under the remaining question, 'When am I?' she wrote [Slide 19]:

A long time ago in Fairy Tale Land.

[Slide 20] *Once Zadie had finished answering all the questions in The Little Story Book she ran over to The Big Story Book and sat down to read the story that now lay within, waiting to be discovered.*

This is the story she found…

Extension activity: story enquiry

I would suggest waiting until the following week, or session, before going on to read / tell *Matilda, The Fireless Dragon*. Use the remainder of this session to explore the nature of stories. This will give the children some reflection time on the subject that they will be thinking about – stories, plots and characters – when they do the 'Once Upon an If' activity on page 97. If you have not done so already, then you may want to use the 'Story enquiry' extension activity on page 102 following the story *The Matches* to begin your enquiry into the nature of stories. If you are using the 'Story enquiry' to follow the story *Once Upon an If* instead of *The Matches* then you may want to consider some of the following ideas / questions in addition:

- Does a story have to have certain kinds of characters?
- What is a *genre*? (The class could be set the task of researching this.)
- What does a genre tell you about what sorts of characters you may have?
- What does the *when* of a story tell you about what can happen in a story? (Can a story that happens 'long, long ago' have cars, for example? If so, how?)

Once Upon an If (part 2)

Starting age: seven years

Themes:
- Stories and stereotypes
- Bluff, knowledge and risk
- Belief
- Sources for belief
- Heroism
- Problem solving

Matilda, The Fireless Dragon

Because *Matilda, The Fireless Dragon* has been magically written by The Story Book, this story has been written in a more literary style. Though I have spent a great deal of time encouraging you to story*tell*, on this occasion I am going to recommend that you read *Matilda, The Fireless Dragon* rather than tell it, although, if you can learn and recall all the jokes then there's no reason why you shouldn't tell it. This story can also be read as a story in its own right. If you decide to do this then simply omit the part at the end that describes Zadie's reaction to the story. This, and the preceding story, can be used to show the children that they do not have to use the conventional stereotypes in their stories, and they can be used to explore plot conventions, standard tropes and clichéd or non-clichéd uses of them. (See Appendix 1 'Quick view steps' *Once Upon an If (part two)* and '*Once Upon an If* classroom activity' on page 97.)

The story

Once upon a time there was a dragon called Matilda. Matilda was a dragon that couldn't breathe fire and she lived in a cave by herself. All she wanted was to be left alone.

But the local townspeople just wouldn't do that. They were always bothering her with one thing or another.

This week it was the Princess. She had recently been bitten by a werewolf, but it was a werewolf that had no teeth so she had not been affected by the 'curse of the werewolf' – which says that if you are bitten by a werewolf, you turn into one! However, she had transformed into something – not because of the werewolf but because she had just turned 13. She had transformed into... a teenager! This meant that, all this week, she had lain in bed until noon and when she did finally get up she would be in a foul mood.

'I would rather DIE than live with YOU, mum and dad!' she screamed as she arrived at Matilda's cave. 'I'm going to chain myself up outside the dragon's cave until it EATS ME! And I DON'T CARE!!'

Oh no! thought Matilda as the Princess chained herself up, I was just drifting off to sleep.

When a handsome knight rode into the town the following day, the King and Queen told him that their beautiful daughter had been kidnapped by the evil dragon that lived in the hills. So the next thing to disturb Matilda was a knight with an over-long lance and a little too much enthusiasm for slaying dragons.

Oh no! thought Matilda again, with a silent sigh.

For the next three days poor Matilda was vexed by the over-zealous knight. But he was unable to slay her.

And it was a good job too.

Because on the fourth day the townspeople were themselves terrorised by a water monster. It had been created by a wizard who had lost control of it and now the huge giant, made entirely of water, was on the rampage, drowning cattle, flattening crops and destroying buildings.

'Our only hope,' said the king, 'is to ask the dragon to help us.'

Matilda was busy fighting the knight who was also busy trying to slay her. Not very effectively, it has to be said. Then the King arrived and told the knight to stop slaying the dragon.

'I have come here today to offer a royal apology,' said the King to Matilda, 'And would you be kind enough to help us repel a water monster that is terrorising our town?'

'Why should I help you?' said Matilda. 'All you've done is cause me misery.'

'I know,' said the King, 'and I'm very sorry. But, in return for your help, we will give you anything you want,' he promised.

'There is one thing I want that you could give me,' said Matilda.

'Name it!' said the King.

'Solitude. I just want to be left alone!'

'It will be done,' assured the King, 'if you can help us.'

'The dragon can't even breathe fire!' exclaimed the knight, who was offended that his knightly services were no longer required.

Matilda flew into the town. And the water monster was there, busy creating geezers to knock down trees.

Task Question 1: What can Matilda do to repel the water monster?

Hint: at these junctures in the session there may well be some good opportunities to communicate to the class some of the ideas involved in the *Once Upon an If* classroom activity explained on page 97. It is at this point that many of the children will try to solve the problem faced by Matilda by introducing extraneous material. One boy once said, 'If she can't breathe fire she might be able to breathe ice, then she can freeze the water monster'. At this point you could explain that this 'is cheating' in a story: bringing in something new that has not been mentioned in order to solve a problem. The idea behind good story writing is that problems are solved with only what has been given at the outset so as not to deceive the audience or readers. Matilda's solution impresses precisely because she solves the problem in spite of her shortcoming; as the audience will find out, she does so through clever, psychological trickery.

Encourage the class to think creatively when they try to solve the problems – they should not feel that they are trying to find 'the right answer', simply to think 'within the rules'. I have had some children correctly identify Matilda's solution ('Matilda may not be able to breathe fire, but the water monster doesn't know that!' said one boy), but from those that haven't, I have heard some very creative alternative solutions. This is good practice for the class's own writing that will follow this story if you do the creative writing exercise.

When the monster saw the dragon swoop down it was somewhat alarmed as dragons are known to breathe large amounts of fire. And if there's one thing a water monster – being made entirely of water – doesn't like very much, it is large amounts of fire!

'Hello!' said Matilda. 'Now, let's get rid of you,' she said as she started to intake a huge breath.

'No! Stop!' shouted the frightened water monster. 'Okay, I'll go.'

But just as the monster was edging its way to leave the town and its people the knight shouted out, still irritated with Matilda, 'The dragon can't breathe fire, you know!'

Task Question 2: Now that the knight has revealed that Matilda cannot breathe fire what can she do?

The water monster stopped in its tracks. Then turned around and looked at Matilda, who was still holding her breath as if she was about to breathe out.

'Is this true?' asked the monster in a gurgly voice.

'Well,' said Matilda, breathing out in a slow, controlled way, 'everyone knows that dragons breathe fire.'

'But he just said that you don't,' said the monster, pointing to the knight.

'Ah, yes, the knight,' said Matilda. 'You see, he doesn't like me very much, so he's just saying that to annoy me.'

The water monster walked threateningly towards Matilda. It was growing less and less afraid of her by the second.

'Do you *really* want to take the risk,' said Matilda after a pause, 'given what you know about dragons? Maybe I can *breathe fire* and maybe I can't. Do you want to find out?'

Task Question 3: What should the water monster think?

Nested Questions:
- If all the dragons the water monster had previously met breathed fire, should the water monster believe that Matilda breathes fire?
- If the water monster had only read that *all* dragons breathe fire, should the water monster believe that Matilda breathes fire?
- If the water monster had read that *most* dragons breathe fire, should the water monster believe that Matilda breathes fire?
- If the water monster had read that *some* dragons breathe fire, should the water monster believe that Matilda breathes fire?
- If the water monster had read that *few* dragons breathe fire, should the water monster believe that Matilda breathes fire?
- If the water monster had read that *it is a myth* that dragons breathe fire, should the water monster believe that Matilda breathes fire?
- Is there something that the water monster can say, or do, to Matilda? If so, what should Matilda say, or do, in return?
- What would be the reasonable thing for the water monster to do?

And with that she took in a huge breath and looked with wide eyes at the monster.

The monster looked back at her, waited, and then… eventually he slowly turned to go.

The water monster had decided it was a risk too great to take.

Once the monster had gone Matilda was able to breathe out, which was good because she was just about to faint.

'Hip-Hip Hooray!!' the townspeople cheered.

Matilda went over to the knight, who had nearly spoilt everything, and said, 'I may not be able to breathe fire but I am big enough to EAT YOU!' She opened her huge jaws and gobbled up the knight in one go.

The princess was quite pleased because she found him annoying. Then she decided that she would move in with Matilda: her 'NBF', as the Princess said, which means 'new best friend'.

Oh no! thought Matilda.

The End.

Zadie closed the book then both sighed and smiled. Matilda didn't get to be left alone, she thought, but at least she was the hero; dragons aren't usually heroes, and Matilda may have been fireless but she certainly wasn't fearless. Then Zadie put her hand on her chin and looked up towards the ceiling; she was already thinking about what she was going to write in The Little Story Book tomorrow…

What if there was a boy who had lost his name? she wondered. And what if there was a cat that couldn't say meow, and what if there was a tree that wished to fly like a bird and…

Further Nested Questions:
- What is a stereotype? (Again, this could be a research task for the class.)
- Are there any stereotypes in this story?
- Does this story challenge any stereotypes?
- Is it okay to use stereotypes in stories? If so, when?

Once Upon an If: story-writing classroom activity

'"Stories don't always have happy endings."
   This stopped him. Because they didn't, did they?... Stories were wild, wild animals and went off in directions you couldn't expect.'
   A Monster Calls – Patrick Ness (2012)

This creative writing classroom activity should be done once you have read the stories *Once Upon an If* and *Matilda, The Fireless Dragon*. The aims of this activity are slightly different, psychologically, from other story-writing exercises. In this exercise the children explicitly create, for each other, the content of the story but then they are asked 'what do you think the story / characters will do now?' This means that rather than asking them what *they* want to happen in your story you are asking them what they think *their story will do* under the conditions that their story partners have set. This means that the story, to some extent, shapes itself.

   Any writer of stories will recognise this special feature of the creative process. Writers will often report how, for example, they can't make a character do something that a particular character wouldn't do (see my comments on the writing of *The Cat That Barked* on page 113). This activity introduces to the young writers a sophisticated aspect to the creative process. The science-fiction writer, Philip K. Dick, when discussing the difference between novels and short stories, wrote,

> 'Anything can happen in a [short] story; the author merely tailors his character to an event. As a writer builds up a novel-length piece... his own characters are doing what they want to do – not what he would like them to do.'
> From a 1968 note in *Beyond Lies The Wub* (1988)

Procedure

1 *Story partner*: Pair-up each member of the class with a 'story partner'.
2 *The Little Story Book*: Have everyone complete the content part of the exercise. Use The Little Story Book template (provided in Appendix 2 on page 215 or it can be accessed by logging on to the online resources that accompany this book) and have everyone fill it out for his or her partner.
3 *Swap*: Have each pair swap the completed Little Story Book template with each other.

4 *The Big Story Book*: Each pupil should then write a story making use of, and adhering to, the information provided by his or her story partner. 'What would your story do?' / 'What would that character do?' – they should try to stay true to their story partner's ideas. They are permitted to change the story ideas only with good narrative reasons. Use the story mountain diagram (see page 220) to help structure the stories.

For an example of how to undertake the first part of the exercise see the *Matilda, The Fireless Dragon* example in Appendix 2 using The Little Story Book: story-writing template on page 215. You can also access these resources by logging on to the online resources that accompany this book.

Extension activity: one word storytelling

This is a well-worn storytelling game that is popular with children and that lends itself perfectly to this activity, because, as the story develops, greater discipline is required as the characters, events etc. determine and limit the story's direction. You may want to run the game before doing the 'Once Upon an If' activity with the class.

1 The children should stand (or sit) in a circle.
2 They must tell a story but each child is only allowed to say one word at a time. The story is told by moving around the circle, successively, from one child to another. They should be encouraged to make use of the characters and plot lines introduced by earlier contributors. This presents the challenge to this game.
3 It could be left entirely to them how the story goes or you may want to 'conduct' by making suggestions or stipulations such as, 'now you need to introduce a second character,' or 'now something needs to happen to 'X', 'Y' and the Z,' and then, 'when we reach this person [indicate] the story needs to end.'

If you play this game regularly you could begin by leaving it up to the children, then, each week, introduce a new element for them to adhere to. I find that they can recall the stories very well, however absurd they get. You could set them the task of writing the story down straight afterwards or you could record it (on a phone or something similar) and write it out for them.

The Matches

Starting age: seven years

Themes:
- The concept of story
- Storytelling skills
- Structure / content
- Scary stories
- Implication

The session around this story invites the children to devise their own story-telling techniques and will allow them to explore the concept of 'story' itself.

Explain to the children that they will be given a special task this week: *to tell a story to someone else*. Explain that they could tell whichever story they like but, to make things easier for them, you are going to give them a 'scary story' to tell that shouldn't be too difficult to remember. Make sure everyone is settled and ready for a story. You could dim the lights to help create an atmosphere before telling them *The Matches*.

Note: I first found this story in the introduction to *Favourite Folktales From Around The World*, edited by Jane Yolen (1987). She says that the story was first reported by the collector Katharine Briggs. In Yolen's book it is even shorter than mine:

'He woke up frightened and reached for the matches, and the matches were put into his hand.'

I have made explicit what is only implicit for the benefit of a younger audience. You may want to refer to Yolen's version when discussing whether it should have more description or less.

When they are ready, tell the children the following story in as lively and interesting a way as you can (without going over the top!):

The story

(I have marked in with a / the beginning, the middle and the end sections. You may want to use these for a later discussion. The children may not agree with this division.)

A long time ago there was a man who lived by himself in a big house. / One night, he awoke sweating and terrified, convinced there was someone else in the room with him. / He searched in the darkness for some matches with which to light a candle... and in the darkness, the matches were handed to him!

Task Question 1: Can anyone say back to the class what happened in the story?

This is not a storytelling task, just a plot-recall task to help embed the story in the minds of the children. You could extend this by asking them to turn to a partner and take it in turns to tell each other what happened in the story. They should correct each other and fill in any gaps. Even at this stage, some of them will naturally story*tell*. The next task is a storytelling activity.

Task Question 2: When you tell this story to someone, how can you tell it so that it will work really well?

In pairs or groups the children should be given a minute or two to think of different ways that they could tell the story effectively. Suggestions I have heard from some Year 3 (age seven to eight) classes have included:

- Lower your tone.
- Use more description.
- Get a friend to make some sound effects while you tell it.
- Turn it into a play.
- Turn the lights down.
- Use hand gestures.
- Put pauses in.
- Speed up at the exciting bit ('He scrambled around for some matches to light a candle...').
- Turn it into a comedy ('...and then his mother's voice said, "Are you still up, you should be asleep!"').

- Give the story an ending. (This makes an excellent discussion point: does it have an ending?)
- One very interesting suggestion was that you should say *when it happened* so that people would know that there were no electric lights, providing a reason to the listener for why he didn't just switch the light on.

Whenever the children make a suggestion ask them to demonstrate it to the class. As the story is so short this should not be too difficult for them to do. If you want to make it solely a story*telling* exercise then stipulate that they are not to change the story in any way. Whether it is a story and whether it can be improved can be a separate discussion.

Some of the above suggestions offered by the children are more controversial than others. It is often a good idea to engage the children in a discussion about the more controversial ones. If someone says 'use more description' or 'give the story an ending' ask the class what they think about this and allow different points of view to be voiced, for example: (Year 3) 'It should have an ending because it's boring if you don't know what happens at the end.' / ' It shouldn't have an ending because it keeps people wondering about who or what is in the room and that's more exciting.' You could use an opportunity like this to explain a distinction between 'an ending' and 'a conclusion' (or 'a finish'): *The Matches* clearly has an ending but it is inconclusive for dramatic reasons.

I offer some of my own basic hints for storytelling to the children (to add to their own, if they haven't already said them):

1 Split the story into three parts: a beginning, a middle and an end (not the same as 'a finish'). Ask the children to say what these are in the story.
2 Suggest that they try not to say 'and then…' between every sentence or event. Demonstrate this by telling the story with 'and thens' and then (!) telling it without them.
3 Insert dramatic pauses between the three sections instead of saying 'and then'.
4 Try telling the story in lots of different ways to find out which way works best (list the suggestions the class has already made).

Leave them with the task of telling the story to others at home and then to report back to you the following week about how their storytelling went and about which storytelling method worked best with their audience. If they told a different story ask them to tell it to the class; avoid saying 'perform it' as this may put some off.

Extension activity 1: story enquiry

This extension activity can either be done after *The Matches*, above, or after *Once Upon an If (Part one)* – see page 85. If using with the latter story then see the additions suggested in the notes for that session.

The following enquiry stimulus came from Dylan (aged seven). Explain that you are going to tell the children another story and then say the following:

Once upon a time, the end.

Task Question 1: Is this a story?

Nested Questions:
- If so, then why? If not, why not? (List criteria as children make their suggestions.)
- What is a story?
- Is there something a story must always have?
- What's the difference between content and form?

Note: As an extension activity for older children introduce the following very short story attributed to Ernest Hemingway to compare and contrast with '*Once upon a time, the end*':

For sale: baby shoes, never worn.

Here are some examples from a Year 3 (age seven to eight) class:

A story has…

- Got to be about something or someone. (Subject)
- Got to begin with 'Once upon a time' and end with 'The end'. (Formal)
- Got to have a problem in it. (Content / tension)
- If you say something (anything!) it's a story.
- Something's got to happen. (Plot)
- More than one thing has to happen. (Plot / sequence)
- There has to be action. (Content)
- It's a story if the teacher says it is. (This was said because I had said 'I'm going to tell you another story'.) Question to the class: 'If I *say* it's a story, does that make it a story?'

As you can imagine many of these ideas generated a great deal of debate. For example, many of the children did not agree that a story is 'anything you say'

('I could just say "was" – that's not a story!' objected one child) and many disagreed that a story is merely formal. Once this enquiry has been conducted return to the story *The Matches* and ask:

> **Task Question 2:** Was that a story? If so, why? If not, why not?

End the session by telling them a longer story (one of your own favourites or one from this book). Invite them to tell the story too, when they go home. (If you do, then don't make it too long.)

Extension activity 2: tell a longer story

1 Take a longer story and chop it up into lots of little bits.
2 Draw a storyboard – little pictures that describe the sequence of events; a picture version of a keyword list (see page 35).
3 Give out the story in bits to pairs of children.
4 Set them the task of learning their bit and telling it without reading it off the page.
5 Tell the story around the whole class.

Extension activity 3: what was it?

Ask the children to say what it was that handed him the matches in each of their own imaginations.
(This could be done as a writing exercise.)
Endings suggested by a Year 3 class:

- a werewolf
- a ghost
- his mother! (comedy ending)
- the air itself
- aliens.

Extension activity 4: stories

Are these examples stories?

- Once upon a time there was a twig.
- Once upon a time they lived happily ever after.
- Once there was a boy. He was happy. Then he wasn't happy. But eventually he was happy again. The end.

- The Hobbit, or There and Back Again (Tolkien, 1937). Is this, the official full title of Tolkien's classic, by itself a story?

Extension activity 5: flash-fiction

There is a name for very short stories such as the Hemingway example above; they're called *flash-fiction*. Here's another example of flash-fiction by the graphic novel author Alan Moore (see Very Short Stories link in bibliography):

'Machine. Unexpectedly, I'd invented a time'

- Set older children the task of writing a flash-fiction short story (perhaps with a word limit: 20 or 100 words, or fewer words each week).
- Can the class say what the story is in Moore's example? For example, can they say:
  - Whether there are any characters?
  - Or goals?
  - Whether any characters achieve their goals?
  - What the genre is?
  - What the subject is?
  - What happens?
  - And any other questions you can think of…

The Boy With No Name

Starting age: seven years (this story works with even younger children too – five and six-year-olds)

Themes:
- Names
- Labels
- Identity
- Formal argumentation
- Self-worth

The story of *The Boy With No Name* is written to be interactive. The children can be engaged as it goes along so I have placed Task Questions at the points where I generally ask my audience questions. They are only suggestions, so you may not want to ask them all in one telling. This story also includes a joke which even very young children seem to 'get': when the boy misunderstands Hannah's claim that her name is the same forwards or backwards. Whether any of the children get it or not may depend on how well the story is read or told. When they do get the joke it dispels the myth that children of a very early age only laugh at 'slapstick' humour such as people bumping into things; they are capable of much more sophisticated humour than many of us might think.

The story

There was once a boy called…

Well, you see, there is a problem with this story because it is about a boy with no name and it is very difficult to tell a story about someone with no name, but I shall do my best.

The boy with no name was deeply unhappy precisely because he was without a name.

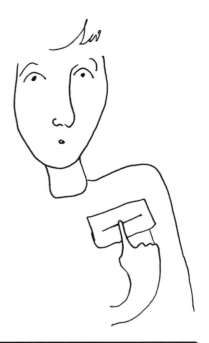

Everyone else used to call him 'Thing-a-ma-jig' or 'What's-his-name' or 'Ooja-ma-flip' but he didn't like those because 'Thing-a-ma-jig', 'What's-his-name' and 'Ooja-ma-flip' are names for people without names.

He thought that someone must have lost his name some time before and so he decided to set out on a quest to find his name again and then he would know who he was and he would be able to answer the question, 'Who are you?'

'Because, if I don't have a name,' said the boy with no name, 'then I'm just nobody!'

Task Question 1: If you have no name then are you just nobody?

Nested Questions:
- How important is your name when saying who you are?
- When is somebody nobody?
- What is a name for?
- What does a name do?
- What would life be like if you had no name?

First, he came across a chair all by itself in the middle of a field.

'How did you get your name, Mr. Chair?' He asked it.

But the chair didn't say anything... because it was a chair!

Some suggested Task Questions:
- How did the chair get its name?
- Is the word 'chair' a name?
- What would happen if a chair didn't have a name?

Then a girl came into the field and sat upon the chair.
'What's your name?' the boy asked her.
'Hannah,' said the girl, 'and my name is very special.'
'Why?' he asked.

Write the name 'Hannah' up on the board.

Task Question 3: Look at the letters of her name very carefully. Can you tell what's special about her name?

Hannah explained why her name is special: 'Because it's the same forwards or backwards.'

The boy said, 'Let's see shall we. Turn around!' Hannah did as she was asked and stood up and turned her back to him. Then he asked, 'What's your name now?' She said, 'It's Hannah.'

'You are right,' said the boy. 'Your name is the same whichever way you stand: forwards or backwards.'

The boy walked on, amazed at such a magical name. He said to himself: 'I wish I could have a name as magical as that.'

Task Question 4: Is that what she meant? If not, then what did she mean? And what did he *think* she meant?

Shortly afterwards, he came across another boy walking the other way. The boy was looking very confused.

'What's your name?' asked the boy with no name.

'I don't know,' replied the other boy.

'What do you mean, you don't know?'

'Well,' he replied, 'my name changes every few minutes so I keep forgetting who I am. It's hard to keep up.'

'Who are you now?' asked the boy with no name.

'I'm George, I think – no, I'm Megdeep now – it's just changed. Who are you?' he asked the boy with no name.

'I don't know because I don't have a name,' explained the boy. 'I think it was lost and I'm on a quest to find it.'

The-boy-whose-name-kept-changing looked concerned and then he said, 'There's something I must tell you: you don't lose names, or find them, names are given to you. That's why my name keeps changing because somebody keeps giving me a different one.'

'Oh no!' said the boy with no name. 'If names are given to you, and not lost or found, that means I'll never have a name. I suppose I should thank you, though, for telling me the truth, erm... Change-a-Name.'

'What did you just call me?' asked the-boy-whose-name-kept-changing.

'Change-a-Name,' said the boy with no name, 'it just came to me.' Then he thought for a moment and then said, 'But, wait a minute! I think I may have found you a name that you can keep. One that won't keep changing.'

'What do you mean?' asked the boy whose name kept changing, who was, by now, looking even more confused.

'If your name changes every few minutes,' explained the boy with no name, 'then something that is always true of you is that your name keeps changing. So, you can always be called 'Change-a-Name' even if your name keeps changing.'

'That's brilliant!' said Change-a-Name. 'I will keep that name forever. Thank you, erm...' Then Change-a-name walked away smiling and singing, now that he had a name that wouldn't change:

'I'm Change-a-name,
I'm Change-a-name
A name that always
Stays the same.

I'm Change-a-name,
I'm Change-a-name
My name will never
Change again!'

The boy with no name was happy to have given someone else a name but still nobody had given him one.

Upon realising that he would never find his name the boy with no name wandered in the other direction still sad and nameless.

A little while later he met a girl playing by the roadside.

'Who are you?' he asked.

'Don't ask me that question!' said the girl.

'Why?'

'Because my name is so long that you will probably fall asleep half way through,' she warned him. 'Most people do.'

'I promise I won't,' said the boy.

'OK. I warned you! My name is:' she took a deep breath, 'Harriettatina Morderwer Halfthwit Bob Iddlewiddle Nintwit Gorsbush Nobblesworth.'

'What?' he exclaimed.

'My name is:' she took another deep breath and then said, slower this time, 'Harriettatina Morderwer Halfthwit Bob Iddlewiddle Nintwit Gorsbush Nobblesworth.'

'I'm afraid I can't remember all that,' said the boy. 'All I can remember is Bob.'

'That's the only bit anyone remembers! And it's a boy's name!' said Harriettatina. 'Who are you, anyway?' she asked eventually.

'I don't know who I am,' answered the boy with no name.

'Why?' she asked.

'Because I don't have a name,' he explained.

'What do you mean you don't have a name? Everyone has a name! Even things that aren't real, like Humpty Dumpty, have a name!'

'I don't and so I sometimes feel like I'm not real,' said the boy with no name, sadly. 'I thought it had been lost,' he continued, 'and I was on a journey to find it but I met a boy called Chang-a-name – well, he wasn't called Change-a-name when I met him but he is now – anyway, he told me that you don't find names, they are given to you, and nobody has ever given me a name. But now I realise that I never had a name and I never will.'

'That's terrible,' said Harriettatina.

'And that's why I'm so sad,' he said.

Harriettatina stopped and thought for a minute. Then she said, 'I have an idea! Why don't I give you one of my names – there are far too many for me.'

'That's a great idea!' said the boy with no name.

He tried on each of her names, one by one, until he found the one that suited him best.

First he tried on Harriettatina. Do you think that name would suit him?

Then he tried on Morderwer. Would that suit him?

What about Halfthwit? Bob? Iddlewiddle? Nintwit? How about Gorsbush? What about Nobblesworth?

Eventually the boy with no name decided which name he liked best.

'Thank you for giving me my name,' he said.

'And thank you for shortening mine,' said Harriettatina, 'Harriettatina Morderwer Halfthwit Iddlewiddle Nintwit Gorsbush Nobblesworth is the perfect length.' They shook hands and both went home much happier than when they had met each other.

When he opened the door to his house his mum shouted, 'Who's that?'

And the-boy-with-a-new-name replied, 'It's me: Bob.'

Task Question: How important is a name?

Nested Questions:
- Can you have a name for people without names such as 'Thing-a-ma-jig'?
- How can something that doesn't exist, like Humpty Dumpty, have a name?
- If you swapped names with someone, would they become you and would you become them?
- If everyone had the same name would that mean that everyone is the same person?
- Why do people suit their names? Does everyone suit his or her name?
- Finish this sentence: 'If nobody had a name then…'
- Did he get the magical name he wanted, like Hannah?
- If you found an object that didn't have a name, what would it be?

Extension activity: whole-class game – who am I?

In this game one person, the player, stands up and has to decide to be someone else in the room, without telling anyone who. The player can be anyone they want – a girl or boy – but it is a good idea that the player secretly tells you, the teacher, who they are so that you can help if they get stuck or forget, and so they don't change who they are during the game. Encourage the player not to choose their best friends, as the others are therefore likely to guess easily. The player then gives one clue about who they are by saying, for example, 'I am a girl'. Then they choose someone (or a number of children) to guess who they are. If the class is not able to guess correctly then they have to say another clue such as, 'I am wearing a blue jumper'. The aim is to get the class to guess who they are in three or less goes by giving only one clue each time. If the class has not guessed who they are in three guesses then it is the end of their go as player and someone else should become the player. It is a good game for identifying unique features.

Once they get the hang of this game you could set the challenge of seeing if there is anyone who would like to have a go at getting the class to guess who they are with just one clue-word for the class. In this case they really have to think of something unique to that person. Someone once said, 'I have grey hair' – Oh, that'll be me then!

The Cat That Barked

Starting age: eight years

Themes:
- Words
- Meaning
- Argumentation
- Language (human and non-human)
- Context

Dialogues have a long relationship with thinking. Probably the most famous philosophical dialogues were those written by Plato approximately 2500 years ago, though the genre has been found even earlier with the *Sumerian Disputations* and the Indian *Vedas*. Almost all of Plato's philosophical writing was written in this form. The word *dialogue* comes from the ancient Greek words *dia* ('through' or 'across') and *logos* ('word', 'speech', 'account'). Dialogue is usually understood to mean 'a conversation or discourse held between two or more individuals', but the etymology tells a slightly different, and more interesting story. Dialogue is simply 'through speech'. This can be understood two ways: either 'something that is done through the medium of speech' and including, therefore, those things that characterise speech, or 'a kind of speech that goes through, across (or penetrates) something'.

Understood in these ways a dialogue can perfectly well be held by one person as they think deeply about something. What distinguishes this kind of dialogue from *thought* or *monologue* is that, though the dialogue is taking place in the head of one person, it's *as if* there were two or more people discoursing. Read the French philosopher Rene Descartes' *Meditations* (1641) for an example of this kind of inner dialogue held by just one person. In his dialogue *The Theaetetus* Plato (Fourth Century BCE) has the character, Socrates, give this the name 'silent dialogue'.

Writing stories like *The Cat That Barked* is a great way to encourage dialogic thinking in a single individual. Interestingly, I had no idea where this dialogue was going when I began it and the cat's insight, that meowing is different from saying 'meow', was unknown to me at the outset. You could say I became convinced by the argument of the cat *as if* the cat was outside my head, not inside. Apart from Plato's many and great dialogues, for other well-known examples of writing where one writer wrestles with conflicting ideas using dialogue, see Andrew Marvell's poem 'Dialogue Between The Soul and Body' (Bate 2005), David Hume's *Dialogues Concerning Natural Religions* (1779) and Berkeley's *Three Dialogues Between Hylas and Philonus* (1713). Stephen Law uses dialogues very effectively to introduce philosophy to a teenage audience in his books *The Philosophy Files* (2011) and *The Philosophy Gym* (2004). As well as the stories, I have included a dialogue version of *The Cat That Barked* so that it can also be performed in class by willing actors. This story is better read than told (see 'Speaking and lifting from the page' on page 28 to help with your reading performance skills.)

The story

'Woof!' barked the cat.

I know what you're thinking: cats don't bark. But this one does. In fact, this is a story about a cat that barked: no matter how hard the cat tried, when it opened its mouth to 'meow', out would bark a 'woof'.

So, let me begin again...

This is the story of The Cat That Barked.

'Woof!' barked the cat.

'What?' said the dog.

'Woof!' repeated the cat. 'Obviously,' the cat continued, 'I mean [spelling] "M.E.O.W." but I can't say that so: woof!'

'Oh, I thought you were going to say something interesting.' Then the dog curled up again to go back to sleep.

'You would say that,' said the cat, 'because I said "woof". Anyway, "M.E.O.W." is just as interesting as "woof".'

'No it's not,' said the dog.

'Yes it is.'

'No it's not!'

The cat sighed, 'Let me put it another way,' he said. '"M.E.O.W." is just as uninteresting as "woof"'

'What do you mean? "Woof" isn't uninteresting. "Woof" happens to be very interesting,' said the dog, beginning to get annoyed with the cat.

'Okay. What does it mean then?' said the cat.

Task Question 1: What does 'woof' mean?

Nested Questions:
- What does 'woof' mean to humans?
- What does it mean to dogs?
- Is speaking about meaning even meaningful or relevant when talking about dogs or cats?
- Do dogs say 'woof'?
- Is 'woof' part of a language?
- Do dogs have a language?
- What is language?

'Erm. Errr... I don't know, err... lots of things. There: it means lots of things. And that makes it very interesting. It's not like normal words that have only one, two or three meanings – at the most. "Woof" can mean anything.'

'And that,' said the cat, 'is precisely why it is uninteresting because if it can mean anything that's the same as it meaning nothing.'

Task Question 2: Can 'woof' mean anything?

Nested Questions:
- Is meaning 'anything' the same as meaning 'nothing'?
- What does the cat mean by this?
- Could you have a language with just one word?

The dog wasn't sure how to respond. So he decided just to poke the cat because he was being annoying.

'Ow!' said the cat. 'That hurt!'

'Don't be so annoying then,' said the dog.

Nobody said anything for a while.

Then the dog said, 'Did you just say "ow"?'

'Who? Me?' said the cat.

'Yes. And did you just say "me"?' said the dog, more excitably.

'Yeah, so what?'

'Well, if you can say "me" and you can say "ow" then you can say "meow".'
The dog looked at the cat, awaiting a response.

The cat looked at the dog silently, but intently.

The dog waited.

The cat looked.

Then the cat said, 'No I can't.'

'Why?'

'Because,' said the cat, '"me" and "ow" are two completely different words
to M.E.O.W. – They mean completely different things: "me" is the first person
singular object pronoun and "ow" is... ow!'

'Yes, but if you can make the sound me and the sound ow then you can put
them together to make me-ow. Try it!'

The cat looked at the dog for a few more seconds. The dog looked back
waiting. Then the cat put his lips together and went, 'Mmmm...' then the dog
said, 'Go on eeeee.'

'...Eeee...'

'And then ow,'

'...Ooowwwa,' finished the cat.

'And then all together,' instructed the dog.

'Mee-oooww.'

'There,' said the dog, 'you can "meow".'

Task Question 3: Can the cat meow?

Nested Questions:
- What is a meow?
- Is there a difference between a meow and saying 'meow'?
- What do you think the cat will say?

'I can say "me" and I can say "ow",' said the cat, 'and I can put them together to
say "me-ow" but I cannot M.E.O.W.'

The dog looked really puzzled.

'Because M.E.O.W.ing is different from saying "me-ow",' explained the cat, 'Humans can say "me-ow" but they can't actually M.E.O.W. It's like snoring: saying "snoring" is not the same as actually snoring.'

'Yeah, you've got a point,' said the dog, conceding unexpectedly.

'Oh. Thanks,' said the cat, surprised that the dog had conceded. And then the cat said, 'and may I thank you again?'

'What for?' asked the dog.

'For helping me to say "me-ow". Sort of.' said the cat.

'That's okay,' said the dog, 'what are friends for?!'

'Woof!' said the cat.

'Woof!' said the dog.

Task Question 4: What does 'woof' mean when the cat and dog say it at the end of the story?

Nested Questions:
- What do you think 'woof' meant at the start of the story when the cat said it?
- How can you work out the meaning of the woofs if you don't already know what they mean?
- How important is context for meaning and understanding of meaning?

Writing dialogues

Despite the dialogue's early dominance, thanks to the French writer Michel de Montaigne (1533–92), who invented the form, academic writing has become dominated by the *essay*. But, arguably, there is something much more natural about the dialogue form, as one can develop ideas more organically. Even if the ideas and insights gained from writing a dialogue are then recast into essay form, I think there is a great deal of value in writing using the dialogue – for all ages. A dialogue should always begin with a question or contentious issue ranging from pressing concerns for the children such as 'is it right that we are not allowed to bring mobile phones into school?' to philosophical issues they may never have thought about before such as 'is the mind the same thing as the brain?'

You should find suitable questions for dialogue-writing after all the stories in the lists of Task and Nested Questions. A simple way to proceed is to have two voices *A* and *B* or *Pro* and *Contra* or *For* and *Against* and so on. Alternatively, the children – particularly older ones – may want to construct a dramatic setting such as a psychologist and a brain surgeon arguing about the mind and brain or a teacher and a child arguing about mobile phone use in schools. They could be more creative and have the dialogue between two characters called Mind and Brain. As well as being a great way to develop thinking, dialogues can also, as with the story above, be a lot of fun. (See also 'The imaginary disagreer strategy' on page 74).

Some ideas for dialogues:

- A conversation between a caterpillar and a butterfly about whether they are the same or different.
- A ghost and a rock about physical and non-physical stuff.
- A girl and a boy about which gender is better, for exploring the issues surrounding gender, but where the girl is arguing for boys and the boy is arguing for girls, both wishing they were the other. (This is an age-appropriate exercise.)

There is a dialogue version of The Cat That Barked available online.

The Patience of Trees

Starting age: ten years

Themes:
- Freedom
- Free will
- Social conditions and mobility
- Aspiration
- Knowledge

This story has been inspired by several stories and images given by philosophers. The story of the river that thinks itself free because it can freeze, flow and evaporate (though it can only do these things under certain very strict conditions) comes from Schopenhauer (1839) in his *Prize Essay on The Freedom of The Will*; the story of the leaf that thinks itself free though borne by the wind is reported to have come from Wittgenstein (Anscombe, 2000). And the image of the tree of knowledge that has become all that it can become, represents Spinoza's idea of *freedom* (Curley, 1994), though he himself denied that we have any *free will*, being, like Schopenhauer, a *determinist*.

I have woven all of these together to create a parable that allows for thinking and discussion on the idea of both freedom, determinism and free will. It also has a few other little references thrown in, such as the Epicurean / Buddhist idea that if you adjust your expectations to meet reality then happiness is easier to reach ('Well, I always want to be where I am, then it's easy to be happy').

Though a parable, this story is not meant to be told as a moral precept for the children to learn. They should be encouraged to critically engage with the notions introduced through the story. For instance, you could ask them, 'Is it true that it's easier to be happy if you want to be where you are? Do you agree with the leaf?' (See 'Making effective use of a moral' on page 64). This story works well told to the end and followed by the Task Question. However, you may want to ask questions as you go. If so, then ask the questions suggested that seem most appropriate.

Keyword list

- weeping willow
- free as a bird
- rooted
- happiness is easy
- frozen
- windy
- The Little Tree
- home again

- The Little Tree rises
- the patience of trees
- the flying seed
- the learning tree
- grateful and happy
- 'But you can't…'
- 'You can only…'
- bloom

The story
Chapter 1

There was once a river, a leaf and a tree. The tree was a beautiful willow and it stood just next to the river. Its branches hung over the bank, the tips of which brushed the surface of the water as if in grief.

The willow was weeping.

'What's wrong?' asked the leaf.

'I'm sad because I watch the birds nest in me and then fly up into the sky. I long to be able to fly like a bird. But I'm not free like a bird because I'm rooted in the ground,' said the tree.

'Poor Tree!' said the river.

'You *are free*,' continued the tree to the river. 'You can do so many things. You can turn solid if you want to, you can flow and you can rise up into the air and fly like a bird. And you, Leaf, can blow this way and that, as you like, just like a butterfly free in the air. I cannot do any of those things.'

(Optional) **Task Question 1:** How is the river able to do all these things?)

'But your roots go so deep,' said the leaf. 'You know things no one else knows. Deep, wise things.'

'But what use is knowing things if you can't do anything with them,' said the tree, 'if you're rooted to the spot.'

The leaf was blown on to a lower branch by a sudden gust of wind. 'Oh,' said the leaf, 'that's just where I wanted to go. I suppose.'

'You always say that,' said the river, 'when the wind blows you.'

'Well, I always want to be where I am,' said the leaf, 'then it's easy to be happy.'

(Optional) **Task Question 2:** Are the leaf and the river free, as the tree supposes?

Nested Questions:
- What do you think of the reasons the tree gives for why the leaf and the river are free and for why the tree is not?
- Is a bird that can fly free?

The next morning it was bitterly cold and the river had frozen over. The people from the nearby town were skating on the river's glistening surface.

'Look how pretty you are!' said the tree to the river.

'Yes, you can see yourself,' said the leaf.

'I wish I could do that!' said the tree.

The next day a fierce wind was blowing and the leaf found itself carried up and up, spiralling into the air, over and under clouds. 'Just like a bird,' thought the tree enviously.

But the leaf had never been blown this far before and when it was finally delivered somewhere it was far, far away from its home with the tree by the river. 'Just... er... where I... er... wanted to be?' said the leaf, looking around to see where it was.

The leaf had landed on the branches of another tree and it was the same kind of tree as the tree the leaf had left. But this tree did not have lots of leaves, it was much smaller, withered and not nearly as tall.

'Why are you so small?' asked the leaf.

The little tree said, 'Because here the soil is not rich and there is not much sunshine or rain, as I am always in the shade.' There was no river next to this tree to quench its thirst and its roots did not go deep, and so this tree didn't have the old wisdom of the leaf's tree.

When the leaf told the tree all about the life it led with its friends the river and the tree, the little tree was sad and it longed to be there too, and though there was no rain, there was what looked like a raindrop falling down its meagre trunk. They talked for some time and became friends.

'I need to go soon and return to my friends,' said the leaf. It just so happened that shortly after the leaf had said this, another wind suddenly scooped it up as if called. There wasn't even time to say 'Goodbye!'

The leaf was carried up and up, spiralling into the air, over and under clouds until it was brought gently onto the surface of a nearby river, and the river carried the leaf on its surface over rocks and under bridges. The leaf wondered if this was the same river and where it would take the leaf. It was the leaf's river and the river carried the leaf safely back to its tree.

But the little tree missed the leaf. It wanted to have friends to talk to. There didn't seem to be anything the little tree could do. But then the little tree had an idea, an impossible idea.

The little tree waited until the dead of night. Then, in the darkness there was the sound of struggling as if something, imprisoned for a long time, was trying to rise up. The sound grew louder and then at the base of the tree it seemed that worms were wriggling out of the ground. But they were not worms, they were the tips of roots.

Through sheer determination and moved by the thought of somewhere better, somewhere greener, the little tree had lifted itself from the ground. It had uprooted. All that was left was for the tree to take its first, slow step and, given how long it would take, for the patience of trees. The little tree may not have had the wisdom of the river tree but it did have a wisdom all its own.

The little tree, however, never made it to the river. It wasn't strong enough. Its dead carcass stands halfway between where it began its journey and the river's edge.

But before it took its last step and bent over, blackened, one of its seeds was caught by the wind and the little seed was carried up and up into the air, and it flew with the birds across fields, under and over the clouds until, at long last, it was brought to the river's edge. There the seed found a home in rich soil where its roots searched deep down into the earth, learning...

Chapter 2

There was once a big, beautiful tree whose branches spread out gratefully. There was also a leaf and a river. One day the tree said, 'I'm happy.'

'Why?' asked the river.

'Because I am free,' the tree replied.

'But you can't do what I can do,' said the river boastfully. 'I can turn solid when I want to, I can flow and I can rise up into the air and fly like a bird.'

'And I,' said the leaf, joining in, 'can blow this way and that, where I want to, like a butterfly free in the air. You cannot do any of those things.'

And the tree said, 'But River, you can only turn solid when it's cold, and you can only flow downwards, and you can only rise when the sun shines on you. You cannot choose what form you take. And Leaf, you only blow where the wind blows you and you can only go where you find yourself. You cannot choose which way you go.'

'So, why are you free then when you're stuck, half buried in the ground?' they both said to the learning tree.

'Because I have become all that I can become and I know all that has nourished me and allowed me to bloom.'

Task Question 3: Who, if anyone, is free in this story?

Nested Questions:
- What is freedom?
- What is free will?
- What makes someone or something free?
- The leaf believes that it is free. Is it?
- The river believes that it is free. Is it?
- At the end the learning tree believes that it is free. Is it?

The Promise-Slippers

Starting age: nine years

Themes:
- Promise-keeping
- Intentionality
- Free will
- Autonomy (self-government)
- Compulsion
- Moral obligation
- Love
- Inner and outer beauty
- Character virtues

This story has been written as a fairy tale resembling the more familiar story *The Frog Prince*; the Grimms' *The Frog King or Iron Heinrich* (Tatar, 2012). Both stories include promises and transformed characters, but whereas *The Frog Prince* sustains traditional notions of love, *The Promise-Slippers*, similarly to William Steig's *Shrek* (1990), challenges those notions and provides opportunities for exploring the notions of love and promising.

The use of the word 'bind' in this story is not arbitrary because it is often used by philosophers to describe the special demand moral obligation makes of us. There are two senses of the word 'bind' in this story: where one cannot do otherwise (such as that animals are *bound* to the cycle of life and death) and where one is able to do otherwise but where a moral obligation suggests that one shouldn't (such as being morally *bound* to an agreement). This idea is captured in the famous words traditionally attributed to Martin Luther: 'Here I stand; I can do no other.' (see Diet of Worms in bibliography.) This double meaning in the story allows the contrast to act as a focal point for thinking around the issue of moral obligation.

Keyword list

- Lira: I promise
- in the woods and wolves
- the elf
- the eggs
- happier
- on the moor – the promise
- the elf again and her vow
- the masked man (Colven)
- unmasked and honoured
- married and 'always'

The story

There was once a girl who was, on the whole, a good person but who found it very difficult to keep a promise. Her name was Lira.

'Will you help me with the chores today?' her mother would ask.

'I'm doing something today. I'll help tomorrow, I promise,' would often be Lira's reply.

'Where is that girl?' her mother would demand the next day, but Lira would have forgotten and gone somewhere with her friends. It wasn't that she wilfully avoided keeping her promises – it was more that she would simply forget. Such was Lira.

Task Question 1: If you break a promise does that mean that you told a lie when you made it?

Nested Questions:
- *TX (see page 7) Promise-breaker 1*: imagine you make a promise but intend never to keep it. With this in mind, now answer the TQ above.
- *TX Promise-breaker 2*: imagine you make a promise, intend to keep it, but, like Lira, forget to honour it. With this in mind, now answer the TQ above.

One day she went out to see her granny who lived on the other side of the woods. Her mother said to make sure that she was back before dark. 'I promise!' she tooted as she left to go. '...because there are wolves in the woods that will eat you up given half a chance,' continued her mother, but Lira did not hear these words.

Later that day – much later – she was making her way back through the woods… and it was dark. Before she was able to find her way out of the woods it had become almost totally dark. She was so lost and unable to see where she was going that she had to stop altogether. 'What am I going to do?' she said out loud to herself.

All she could do was to find a big, sheltering tree, curl up under it and wait for the morning light. A little while later she heard a noise that woke her. It was the sound of something moving in the darkness all around. A cloud crossed the sky, uncovering the moon for a moment. As the moonlight fell between the trees it lit up the eyes of many wolves that had, by now, surrounded her. Then the light was lost behind another cloud, and, although it was too dark to see, the wolves knew she was there because they could smell her. And they were hungry.

Just then a small branch fell from the tree under which she was huddled. She looked up to see – what appeared to be – a lamplight descending the tree. Just as the light was above her head a hand appeared from above accompanied by a small voice, 'If you want to live, reach for my hand and pull yourself up.' Lira didn't see that she had much choice.

She was led up the tree by a very small man-like creature that, once they were high up, invited her through a narrow doorway that took them into the tree. Inside was a room; and a cosy-looking room it was too. The creature appeared to be some kind of elf. He made her some tea and offered her some cake. Then he sat down and began to ask her why she was out in the woods all alone, at this time of night. She told the elf the whole story. 'So, you're a promise-breaker, are you? And that's what got you into trouble, isn't it? Well, I may be able to help you with that!' Then the elf sprang up and started to rummage through his things, apparently looking for something.

Eventually the elf said, 'Ah-ha! Here we are!' and he handed Lira the most exquisite pair of shoes she had ever seen. 'You've seen slippers before, haven't you?'

'Yes,' said Lira.

'Well, these are what I call "promise-slippers",' said the elf. 'If you are wearing these shoes when you make a promise then you will have no difficulties keeping to your promise. There! That should solve your problem.'

'Oh, thank you!' she said to the elf.

The next morning she left, clutching her promise-slippers under her arm, having thanked the elf again and having said goodbye. When she returned home, her mother was so relieved to see Lira she told her off and sent her to her bedroom without any food, but not before she had smothered her daughter in kisses. Such is the way of parents.

The promise-slippers were so pretty that Lira wore them wherever she went. A few days later, her mother said to her, 'When you come home from school today, could you remember to collect some eggs from the farmer for me?'

'Of course,' said Lira.

'Now promise me!' her mother instructed.

'I promise,' said Lira without really thinking about it.

'We'll see,' muttered her mother.

They would see.

Of course, with all the fun she was having with her friends on the way home, Lira had completely forgotten about her promise. But as she passed the road that led to the farm she was supposed to visit, her feet stopped walking and they stood her still. 'I can't walk,' she said to her friends, who were looking at her, wondering why she was suddenly stationary. Just then, her legs started walking again but not in the direction she wished them to go; they started marching her down the road towards the farm, all by themselves. And then she remembered: 'The promise-slippers!' she thought. 'They must be making me keep my promise to my mother.' Once she had collected the eggs her legs became her own again.

Everyone was much happier: her mother, father and friends could now rely on Lira to fulfil her promises and Lira could finally become the kind of person she had always wished she could be. She also noticed that it made no difference whether she took off the shoes; if she had been wearing them when she made a promise then her legs would march her to fulfil it.

Task Question 2: Is Lira now a better person?

Nested Questions:
- Should she feel pleased with herself?
- What gives a promise its value?
- If you can't help but keep a promise is it valuable?
- Does the keeping of a promise have to come, willingly, from the person or not?
- Or, is all that matters that the promise is fulfilled?
- Is Lira 'fulfilling' or 'honouring' her promises now that she has the shoes? What is the difference between fulfilling and honouring?
- What kind of person should you wish to be? (See Ethics through narrative on page 12.)

- Make a list of ten characteristics you think you should wish to have. For example:
  - fair
  - strong
  - honest
  - cunning and so on.
- Once you have made your list discuss with a partner whether the characteristics you have each chosen are characteristics you should wish to have.
- The instruction was not 'Make a list of ten characteristics that you wish to have' but 'Make a list of ten characteristics that *you think you should* wish to have.' What is the difference between the two formulations of the instruction?
- What can you do to become the kind of person you should wish to be? Take your list and address each characteristic with recommendations for how to cultivate it. For example: 'To be fairer I need to think about other people's needs and wants more and not just my own; to be stronger I need to do more exercise…'

One day, when Lira was crossing the moor, returning from fulfilling a promise to her mother, she wandered into one of the hidden bogs that her mother was always warning her of. Most were not very dangerous and she could pull herself from them without too much trouble, though she might lose a shoe or two. But she was wearing her promise-slippers, which she loved dearly and on which she relied so much. But however much she tried to escape the bog she could not do so without having to lose her precious promise-slippers. And by the time she realised that she would have to let them go, it was too late and she was up to her thighs in the mud.

When she was up to her neck, and just as she thought that it was going to be all over, a man rode past on a horse. 'Help!' she managed to shout, though with a weak voice. The man stopped, dismounted, knelt down beside her and, after assessing the situation, he said, 'If I free you from the bog will you promise to marry my son ten years from now?'

If she refused, then she would surely die. 'Yes! Yes, of course,' she said quickly, 'I promise.' The man reached out and pulled her from the cloying mud. 'Where do you live?' asked the man. 'I shall come and look for you in ten years' time.' She looked down at her feet. The promise-slippers were gone, claimed by the bog, though she was unsure whether she had still been wearing them when she had said, 'I promise.' But she thought she probably had been as she thought she must have been pulled from them by the man after she had made her promise.

'There really is no need,' said Lira as she realised what had very probably happened. 'I will find you. I promise.'

The man said, 'I am sure you will honour your promise but, for my peace of mind: tell me where you live.'

Task Question 3: Should she honour her promise to the man on the moor?

Nested Questions:

- Should you honour your promises?
- Are there any promises that you should not honour?
- Are there any circumstances under which a promise no longer needs to be honoured?
- Are there any circumstances under which a promise *should* no longer be honoured?

Five years later a local lad, whom she liked very much, asked her to marry him, but Lira remembered her promise to the man on the moor. She had managed to find the elf again that had given her the promise-slippers in the first place and he had told her that she might only be released from the promise 'by the person to whom you made the promise or to whom the promise binds you'. But she had no idea where she could find the man or even who he was. She reasoned that if she were to marry now, then in five years' time – if she had indeed been wearing the promise-slippers when she had made the promise – she would dishonour the marriage, whether she wanted to or not. For this reason, she resolved never to marry until the ten years had passed; when she would be sure that she was either bound by or free of the promise.

A month before the tenth year, a man, covered from head to toe in black and whose face was also covered up with a mask, knocked on the door of her house. Her father let the man in.

'I have come to remind your daughter of a promise she once made to my father, who is now dead,' said the masked man.

'What promise is this?' asked her father of Lira.

Lira told the story of what had happened on the moor but she did not mention the promise-slippers. 'It is your choice, Lira,' said her father, 'whether you honour your promise or not.' Then he left.

Lira knew that it was, very likely, not her choice.

'I will go with you,' she agreed. She had been saddened to discover that the man to whom she had made the promise was now dead, as Lira believed that it meant she could never be released from the promise. The little hope she had held on to all these years was gone.

Task Question 4: Does Lira have a choice?

Nested Questions:
- What is a choice?
- Can she make a choice even if she is not able to enact it (do it)?
- Does the death of the man's father mean that she can never be released from the promise? (See the elf's words explaining how she may be released from the promise.)

Lira accompanied the masked man back to a castle. On the journey they talked a great deal; she found that he was very easy to talk to. He told her that his name was Colven, and that his father had longed for him to marry. 'Then why have you never married all these years?' she asked him. 'Are you married?'

'No,' he said.

'Are you poor?' she asked.

'No.'

'Then why have you not married?' she asked, not sure she wanted to hear the answer.

He said nothing but simply removed the mask that covered his face, behind which was the ugliest, most disfigured face she had ever seen that in no way matched the gentle voice that issued from it. Now she understood why the man on the moor had made her make the promise she had.

She took a deep breath and said, 'I will fulfil my promise. I will marry you.'

Moved by her integrity Colven said, 'I have waited a long time to meet you and to hear you say those words, but now that I have met you I cannot make you go through with something you do not wish to do.' Then he said, 'I release you from your promise.'

Lira burst into tears. 'You don't understand,' she said. 'You cannot release me.'

'What do you mean?' he asked.

So Lira told him the whole story, as best she could, from the beginning. As she drew towards the end of the story she felt herself drawn to Colven in a way she did not understand, but was beginning to. When she finally finished, he once again said, 'I release you,' but then added, 'because I love you.'

She looked at him, this time not with her eyes but with her heart, and what she beheld was beautiful, noble.

They married on the day of the tenth year since her promise to Colven's father; the day to which her promise had bound her. One day, Colven said to her, 'Will you always love me?' and – such is the way of love – Lira said, 'Always. I promise.'

Task Question 5: Did she keep her promise? If so, why?

Nested Questions:
- Do you think she was wearing the promise-slippers when she made her promise to Colven's father?
- Why did she marry Colven?
- Did she fulfil her promise? a) If she married him willingly, through love, then would she have fulfilled her promise? b) If she had married him unwillingly, but out of duty, then would she have fulfilled her promise?
- Was she released from her promise?
- The elf said that she may only be released from the promise 'by the person to whom you made the promise or to whom the promise binds you'. Who does this imply she may be released from her promise by? a) To whom did she make the promise? b) To whom is she bound by the promise?
- Did the promise-slippers make her marry Colven?
- Do you think she will keep her promise that she makes to Colven at the very end of the story to always love him?
- Do you think she should make this promise?
- Is it a promise anyone is able to make? Is it a promise anyone is able to keep?
- Is love for always?
- Can you know how long you will love someone for?
- Are you in control of whether you love someone or not?
- What does it mean when people say, 'A promise is a promise'?
- What is a promise?
- Is a promise different from a deal?
- Is a promise different from an agreement?
- Is a promise different from a contract?

The Six Wise Men

This story demonstrates how you can manipulate the structure of a story to get the most out of it from a thinking point of view. I have already talked about how involving the audience in the story engages the audience effectively, drawing them into the story literally as well as figuratively. This version of the story involves the audience by requesting that they too meet the Maharaja's challenge. This story also has elements inserted in order to pre-empt children's objections; see the section where the six wise men suggest that the Maharaja may be tricking them. I added this because it was something many classes suggested.

This traditional story tells of six (or sometimes three) men who are, in some versions, blind and, in others, blindfolded. The men come into contact with an elephant and then try to find out what an elephant is. Each sightless man encounters a different part of the elephant and falsely concludes that the elephant is like the part of it that they have encountered: the trunk, the leg or the tusk and so on. This is a version of *the fallacy of composition / division*. The story has been used to make many points and lessons in many cultures (see Blind men and an elephant in bibliography for a Wikipedia link). I would like to show how playing with the structure of a well-known story, such as this, can help you to engage your audience actively in a thinking issue.

The aim with this lesson plan is to use the story of 'The Blind Men and The Elephant' to bring the class to thinking about part-whole relationships. In philosophy this is known as 'mereology' (from the Greek 'meros' for part) and it is an ancient tradition that goes back at least as far as the philosopher Aristotle, who famously almost said: 'The whole is different from the sum of its parts.' (This being a more well-known – and catchy – paraphrase of something Aristotle said in Metaphysics Book 8, Fourth Century BCE.) The key insight here is that a certain kind of unity of parts creates something that is more than just its parts. Think of a heap of sand and compare it with something more complex. A heap of sand is just a collection of sand particles but a certain arrangement of molecules and atoms, for instance, can create more than just a collection of molecules and atoms, it can create a thinking, conscious being such as me or you. Though the aims of the session are unaffected by the class knowing that it is an elephant that is in the tent, I usually request that those who have heard the story before don't tell the others what they think (or know) is in the tent. This is just to optimise the class's engagement and enjoyment.

This story gives you an opportunity to mime what it is each wise man encounters when he enters the tent. Close your eyes as you tell this part and show, with your hands, what you describe. (See 'Movement, gestures and expression' on page 42 and 'Physicalisation' on page 44.) This story also affords many opportunities to explore the notion of knowledge. To develop this theme further, see the Nested Questions and extension activities at the end of the chapter.

The story

A long time ago in India there were six wise men and each of the wise men thought he knew everything there was to know. News of their great knowledge travelled far and wide throughout India until the news reached the ears of the Maharaja – which means 'king'. He decided to offer a test to the six wise men to see if they really were as clever as everyone – and they – thought. In the message he added that thousands of people would attend so if they did not accept his invitation they would risk damaging their reputations.

Upon hearing about the Maharaja's test the wise men all arrived at his kingdom as they did not want to be seen as cowards. He showed them a huge tent that he had erected in his courtyard and told them that all they had to do was to tell him what was inside the tent.

'That will be easy,' said one of the wise men.

The Maharaja replied, 'Well, of course it will be easy, if you know all there is to know.' He then explained how the test was to be conducted. The tent was as big as a house and around the outside were six doorways into the tent.

(Draw an aerial view diagram of the tent and its doorways on the board.)

The wise men would each go into a different doorway but they would all be blindfolded before they entered. They would only be able to discover what was inside the tent by touch.

'But this should not be a problem for you,' said the Maharaja, 'As you all know everything there is to know.'

'Indeed!' replied another of the wise men.

The first of the wise men was blindfolded then he entered through the first door. Once inside the tent he immediately bumped into something large and flat that stood in his way. He reached with his hands to discover that whatever it was stood as far as he could reach in all directions. He came out of the tent, satisfied, and said, 'I know what's in the tent. It's a wall.' [Write this up on the board.]

Also blindfolded, the second wise man then entered through the second door. He could feel something very different. In his hands he held something long and thin and flexible that felt rough to the touch with a frayed end. When he emerged from the tent he declared: 'It's rope in the tent!' [Write this up, too.]

Upon entering the tent through the third door the third wise man felt something long, thin, smooth and hard that bent slightly as it came to a sharp point. 'It's a spear! A bent one, but a spear nevertheless,' he told the King. [Write it up.]

The fourth wise man discovered something large and flappy that felt leathery and was high up off the ground. 'It's a flag on a pole,' he said. [Write it up.]

The fifth wise man could not understand how it could be a flag because what he found was solid and cylindrical and came up out of the ground; it was very hard and rough. 'It is a tree trunk, or maybe a tree,' he said. [Write it up.]

Finally, the sixth wise man made his way into the tent. He felt something long, slippery and bendy. He came running out of the tent and screamed, 'It's a snake! I hate snakes! Aaagh!' [Write it up.]

So the first wise man thought it was a wall that was in the tent, the second wise man thought there was rope in there, the third thought the Maharaja had put a bent spear in the tent, the fourth a flag, the fifth a tree, and the sixth wise man thought he had met a snake.

The list should now look like this:
1 a wall
2 a rope
3 a spear
4 a flag
5 a tree trunk
6 a snake

Task Question 1: How many things do you think are in the tent?

Insist that the children do not – at this stage – say what they think is in the tent. You will need to use the *anchoring* technique a good deal here (see 'If it, anchor it, open it up' on page 74).

Nested Questions:
- Does it *have* to be six things or could it be one thing?
- If there is a wall, a rope, a spear, a flag, a tree trunk and a snake in the tent all tied together then would that be one thing or six things?
- If you were to build a robot you would begin by having lots of different bits but when you have finished there is one single robot. So, is the robot one thing or many things?
- If you have a man holding a spear how many things are there? If you have a *statue* of a man with a spear, then how many things are there?
- If there were six different types of tree in the tent could that be one thing (they are *all* trees) or six things (six *types* of tree)?

The six wise men stood there arguing about what they thought was in the tent for a long time:

'How can what I felt possibly be a flag?' 'How can something thin and flexible

block my way?' Until, after a while of arguing like this, one of them said, 'Hey, maybe the Maharaja is trying to trick us and maybe there are six different things in the tent.' They all turned to the Maharaja and said, 'Are there six different things in the tent?'

'No,' replied the Maharaja, 'there is only one thing *in the tent and you have all touched the same thing. So, tell me what it is in order to pass the test.'*

The six wise men all looked at each other quite puzzled as to what was in the tent. What one thing could it be that would fit all the descriptions they had given? The first of the wise men dug his heels into the sand, then said, 'It is a wall.' The second also dug his heels into the sand before he said, 'It is a rope.' The third did the same as he said, 'It is a spear.' The fourth, fifth and sixth wise man each dug their heels in before stating clearly that it was 'a flag,' 'a tree trunk,' and finally, 'a snake!'

Task Question 2: What one thing do you think is in the tent that would fit all the descriptions given by the six wise men?

Nested questions:
- Could it be a changing thing?
- Is it possible that it is one thing that does not change or would it have to change?

Once all the wise men had said what they thought was in the tent the Maharaja gave the order for the tent to he raised. A host of soldiers pulled on some ropes at the side of the tent. When the tent had risen a few feet off the ground they could all see what appeared to be four tree trunks, two at the front and two at the back, standing under the tent:

If no one in the class has guessed that it is an elephant, allow them to have another guess by anchoring them with TQ 2 again (it is not essential that they get it right; they may get something very close, like a dragon). As the tent is lifted you could give them another clue if necessary and / or draw another illustration on the board that reveals a little more information. If someone does say that they think it is an elephant then get the class to check it against the six descriptions, writing each thing next to the original claim:

- a wall – body
- a rope – tail
- a bent spear – tusk
- a flag – ear
- a tree trunk – leg
- a snake – trunk.

Eventually the tent was raised and it was revealed that inside the tent was... an ELEPHANT! None of the wise men had guessed that it was an elephant so the Maharaja said to them that this test had proved that they did not, after all, know all there was to know.

Task Question 3: It was an elephant that was in the tent. So, was it one thing in the tent, six things or another number of things?

Nested Questions:
- How many things is an elephant?
- How many different parts are there to an elephant?
- How many different parts does one part of an elephant have? For instance, how many different parts does a leg have?
- How many things are you?

Extension activities

- (Make up a stick person for this exercise.) If you have a 'stick person' made up of four pencils, a book and a bowl, then how many things are there? Is it *six* things (all the parts added up)? Is it *three* things (all the kinds of things used, i.e. pencils, book, bowl)? Or is it *one* thing (the stick man)? Or is it seven things (the six things it's made of plus the one thing they make). Or another number of things?
- *Feely-bag game*: This is particularly good for younger children. One child puts their hand into a bag with an object in it. They have to get the class to guess what's in the bag but they can only describe how it feels, for example, 'It's hard and curvy. It's long and thin...' and so on.

Task Question 4: How, if at all, would the six wise men come to know everything?
- Is it possible to know everything?
- Is it wise to think you know everything?
- If they had worked together, could they have discovered what it was in the tent?
- If you knew everything about how to ride a bike, *but you had never ridden a bike,* would you be able to ride a bike when you tried for the first time?

The Fair Well

Starting age: five years

Themes:
- Fairness
- Fear
- Wishes

This story takes what I call a *Twilight Zone* approach, inspired by the 1960s television series of the same name that delivered – what were then – popular short stories of the kind that were being published in pulp science fiction and fantasy magazines. This kind of story is often characterised by ending surprisingly, either with a twist or inconclusively. (See 'Stories with a twist' in 'Types of story' on page 5.) Even though there were no regular characters or settings in the series, what seemed to unify the stories was the way in which they were told. They often took a perfectly ordinary situation and then turned it on its head through the introduction of a character, device or inexplicable occurrence – a *novum* (see 'Types of story' on page 5).

These are classic examples of what are known more generally as *What if?* stories (see 'Types of story' on page 5) and are closely related to the more scientific and philosophical *thought-experiment* (see 'Types of story' on page 5 and 'Stories and thought-experiments' on page 17). Thought-experiments are designed specifically for thinking so the similarity between *What if?* stories and thought-experiments shows why *What if?* stories are so suited to thinking with. Many *Twilight Zone* stories use the 'Careful what you wish for!' theme, and that is what *The Fair Well* does, though without the moralistic downfall of the main character that the television series often had.

Many children hold the belief, pre-reflectively, that fairness is 'getting what you want'. Using this *What if?* story we are able to ask, 'Okay! What if you did get what you want? Would that be fair?' We are able to test the class's intuitions about what is fair against the events of the story. This is a perfect example of how thought-experiments work. (See 'Stories and thought-experiments' on page 17.)

Storytelling hint: use your hands to help the class understand the unusual word 'undulated': as you say it, describe, with your hands, a hill with an undulating descent. (See 'Vocabulary' on page 50.)

The story

Mary had been coming home from school each day that week thoroughly miserable. 'It's not fair!' she had exclaimed to her mother at the close of each school day.

'What's not fair?' her mother had asked each time.

'Miss never chooses me,' Mary had said.

'Now, I'm sure that's not true,' her mother had tried to reassure her.

'It is true. She never chooses me. It's not fair!' There seemed to be nothing her mother could say to change her mind.

(Optional) Task Question 1: Is Mary right, is it not fair?

Nested Questions:
- If she has never chosen her then is it not fair?
- If she has only chosen her once is it not fair?

In order to take Mary's mind off whatever it was that was troubling her, her mum decided to take her to a special place that weekend for a picnic. On Saturday they packed up a delicious picnic and drove to the country. It seemed to take hours. 'We must be a long, long way away from the city now', thought Mary. When they arrived at their destination Mary was spellbound by the beauty of the spot her mum had chosen. They laid their picnic on a blanket in the middle of a sloping hillside that undulated its way down to a stream at the bottom of a valley. The sun sparkled through the running water that flowed beneath an old wooden bridge; the whole place seemed to be enchanted, as if magical. On the other side of the bridge was a dark, but also enchanting, wood. After finishing her picnic Mary asked her mum if she could go and play by the bridge. 'Only if you promise not to wander off into the wood; make sure you can always see the bridge,' said her mum. 'I promise,' Mary replied as she trotted happily down to the bridge.

For a while she played by the bridge as she had promised but then she found herself gravitating towards the wood. As she stood by the wood and stared inside she felt an irresistible urge to go inside. Then she thought, 'as long as I don't lose sight of the bridge I'll be safe'. So, she started to make her way into the wood, step by step. After a short while she looked back to make sure she could still see the bridge and hear the running water. There it was. 'Surely I can go a little deeper,' she thought and she ventured further into the wood. She stopped again to check for the bridge and the sound of the water. Just then, a beautiful little butterfly suddenly appeared around her head. She tried to catch it but it was too quick and fluttery. Without thinking, Mary found herself chasing its random movements. A minute or two later it was gone; lost in the darkness. She remembered the bridge and looked around her but she could no longer see it, or the light at the edge of the wood, or hear the sound of the stream. She tried to retrace her steps but found that she could not. There was no pathway under her feet. She realised that she was lost.

As she stood there wondering what to do and starting to feel a little scared, up ahead she noticed another light. She thought it must be the edge of the wood again but when she went towards it she found something very different. There was what seemed to be a magical light issuing from a well, which – oddly – stood in the middle of the wood with no path leading to it. On it there was a sign that read, 'wishing well' across the top. By now she was no longer scared; simply filled with a feeling of wonder. She took out a coin from her pocket and threw it into the well. Thinking back to her miserable week at school she silently wished her wish.

(You may want to ask the class what they think she will have wished for.)

The moment she had finished she heard her mum's voice in the distance, 'Mary!' She shouted back, 'Mum!' and they kept shouting to each other until, at last, they were reunited. Her mum took her into her arms and said, 'Thank goodness you're safe! You must never go off like that again! Do you hear!' But Mary wasn't really listening. She was trying to tell her mum all about the well and its magical glow.

Back at school on Monday, in the morning during register, her teacher Miss Slocombe asked if there was anyone who wanted to volunteer to take the register to the school office. Everyone's hand went up. Miss Slocombe then said…

(Leave a pause and allow the audience to anticipate (see 'Pace and Pause – Audience Anticipation' on page 32) what will happen next.)

'Mary, would you like to do it?' Mary jumped up with a big smile on her face. After all, this was what she had wished for when she was at the wishing well in

the wood. Later on, another errand needed doing. Everyone's hands went up again. And Miss Slocombe chose… (Pause, as above) *Mary. And then again… Mary. It went on like this all week.*

On Friday, when Mary came out of school to meet her mum at the school gates she had a huge, beaming smile. Her mum said, 'How was school this week?' and Mary said, 'It was great. Everything is fair now!'

Task Question: Now that Mary is being chosen, is it fair?

Nested Questions:
- If this isn't fair, what would make it fair?
- Is fair 'getting what you want'?
- Is fair 'everyone getting what they want'?
- Is it possible for everyone to get what they want and it still be fair?
- What is fair? (What does 'fair' mean?)
- What do you think of the following definition for 'fair': 'fair is the right thing to do when the circumstances have been considered'?

Water People

This original story is an allegory inspired by the water cycle, and following a long tradition of 'astronomical allegories', but it also addresses life cycles more generally, birth and death. The story provides an approachable way of dealing with the – sometimes difficult – issue of death and can be used either to introduce the life / water cycle or to test the class's understanding of them after they have completed the module. This is, by the way, a good general way to use enquiries: before a learning module is commenced, in order to assess what children know and don't know about a topic; and / or at the end of a learning module in order to assess how well the class has assimilated what they have learned and how they are able to apply the concepts involved in the topic.

The story

There was once a man made of water and he was born in the mountains. There he stayed for a long time until, having grown lonely in the mountains, he longed for the company of people.

He set out and descended the mountains in search of people.

Eventually the Water Man joined the people of the earth and helped them when he could. When they were thirsty he would provide them with drink. When they were hungry he would water their fields. When, on occasions, he grew angry, he would flatten their houses.

And if he slept for too long they would die of thirst.

Though the Water Man was happy to have found people he sometimes felt sad because they took him for granted. He sometimes felt like the people looked straight through him, as though he wasn't there. They would curse him when there was too much water and they would curse him when there was too little. The Water Man seemed never to be able to please the people of the earth.

Maybe because of this, he sometimes longed to return to the sky where he had come from before he was born in the mountains.

One day he became angry and destroyed many houses in his rage. The people became angry and cursed him. They all gathered together and trapped the Water Man, taking him out into the blazing sun in the middle of the day. Now, because the Water Man is made of water he cannot stay under the sun for long. But the people were angry and they held him under the sun though he pleaded with them to stop. After a time, the Water Man was gone, melted away into the air. He had finally returned to the sky and achieved what he had longed for.

From the sky, he still helps the people when he can, even though they were so angry with him they melted him away; he still waters the fields and provides them with drink and still occasionally gets angry; and people still curse him when it rains and curse him when the rains fail.

Some time after the Water Man left the people of the earth, a woman is born in the mountains and she too is made of water. She too eventually longs for the company of people due to the maddening loneliness of the mountains, and when she wanders down to the people they say to her, 'You have been here before, but as a man.' Of that, however, the Water Woman has no memory.

The Concept Box is a good procedure to use with this story (see page 77), or simply read or tell the story and allow the children to reach their own Emergent Enquiry. Here are some questions anyway that you may find useful, any of which may be used as Task Questions:

Suggested Task Questions:
- Did the Water Man die?
- What is death?
- What is a person?
- What / who is the water man and woman?
- What is a metaphor?
- Is this story a metaphor? If so, a metaphor for what?
- What is an allegory? How is this story an allegory?
- Is the water woman the same person as the water man?
- When someone dies what happens to them?
- What is loneliness?
- Can you find the water cycle in this story?

Flat Earth

Before reading this you may want to read my comments on 'permissible lies' in 'As if: truth and lies in fiction' on page 8. This session is based around the curriculum themes *earth, sun and moon* and *direct and indirect evidence*. In this session the teacher role-plays the ancient Egyptian thereby giving a dynamic and responsive voice to this figure of antiquity. The children role-play the time traveller, so you will need to think on your feet to be able to respond appropriately to the children's arguments and challenges. Their job is to demonstrate to the ancient Egyptian that the Earth is round and not flat. However, given that most of the evidence we have for this is only indirect, it is harder than they will at first think. For instance, if the children say 'that you just have to look in any book!' then you – as the ancient Egyptian – can say something like, 'Ah! But how do you know that the books speak the truth?' or, 'But all of the books in the Pharaoh's library state quite clearly that the Earth is flat'. It may take them a minute or two to work out what is meant by this.

Most direct evidence supports the view that the Earth is flat and this is precisely why this view was historically held by so many for so long: for instance, any landscape or horizon will not appear curved when observed from a ship. This often surprises the children but it is good if they start to realise for themselves that there are these difficulties, through a session like this rather than simply being told.

Aristotle (384–322 BCE) used the apparent movement of the constellations to speculate that the earth was in fact spherical and, later, Eratosthenes (276–195 BCE) surmised its shape by the angles cast by sunbeams.

He also calculated the circumference of the Earth on this basis with remarkable accuracy. I have heard children also make some compelling arguments such as, 'If the Earth was flat then when we look out across the sea we would be able to see America, on a clear day,' or that 'because ships disappear behind a horizon it shows that the Earth must be curved'. Of course, they would need to actually see these things before the arguments could be demonstrated, but the key thing is that these primary-aged children have thought of something that both they and the Egyptian could, in principle, perform and observe. It is therefore the sort of idea that shows a move away from the unreflective and unsupported assertion that 'the Earth must be round because thinking that it's flat is just *stupid!*' This comment is closer to how they can sometimes begin the debate.

This story provides an example of how the second person (see 'Persons: first, second or third?' on page 26) and the present tense (see 'Tenses' on page 25) can be used effectively in storytelling.

The story

You are a time traveller. And also a scientist and historian, specialising in ancient Egyptian languages and the history of science. You have decided to take a trip back in time using a time machine. Given your special interest in ancient Egypt you set the controls of your time machine for ancient Egypt: the year 2500 BCE, to be precise. [You could ask the class how long ago they think this would be.]

When the whirring and humming of your time machine finally stops you open the door and step outside. All your knowledge, and the reading you have done of this time, cannot prepare you for what you see when you actually arrive in ancient Egypt. What particularly strikes you is how new everything looks. And the colours! The statues and pyramids are not mere bare stone, they are coloured and some are even decorated. Quite amazing!

Being a scientist you seek out another who will share your interests. There aren't really any scientists in the sense that there are in your time, but you are able to find a person who is interested in similar things: in how things are and how things work. His name is Amun and once you get the hang of speaking a language you have only had to read before now, the two of you speak at length about a great many things such as cosmology (that is 'the origins of the universe') and the engineering skills and plans that were used to build the pyramids. You are amazed to discover that all the theories modern people have come up with about how the ancient Egyptians built the pyramids are all wrong – you can't wait to get home to write the definitive paper all about it!

Extension activity: research

Have the class research the various theories put forward about how the Egyptians actually engineered the building of the great pyramids such as the 'inside-out theory'.

Among the many things you talk about together you eventually come to the topic of the shape of the Earth. As you already know, the ancient Egyptians believed that the Earth was flat, not round as we think today. They also believed that it rests on a sea that stretches on forever in all directions.

Task Question: How will you persuade Amun that the Earth is in fact round and not flat? Can you?

(At this point the teacher should assume the role of Amun the Egyptian and enter into a role-played dialogue with the children – see above.)

Nested Questions:
- How do you know the Earth is round?
- Does the Earth look round?
- Could the Earth be flat and not round? Could you be wrong in thinking that it is round?
- More advanced question: Does the ancient Egyptian hypothesis (alternative word: *idea*) that the earth rests on an infinite sea make sense? *Note:* Amun, when he understands what we think, may object that our understanding is no different from his: we also posit (or are left with the problem of) an 'infinite sea' of space instead of water; but, in principle, he may say, it's the same idea.

Extension activity in second person stories: putting your class in a story

If your class is of an appropriate age, introduce the children to *Fighting Fantasy Gamebooks* (see Jackson and Livingstone, 2003) or any similar kind of book in which the reader is the protagonist and who decides the path the book takes. Once they understand how the books work, they could be given the task of writing a story that uses the same format.

It

Starting age: five years

Themes:
- Language – indefinite article / pronoun / proper name
- Reference and meaning
- General and particular
- Unknown referents
- Description
- Mystery
- Secrets

It is good to allow the children to engage with this story as it goes along. Stop from time to time to allow questions, comments and points to be raised, or said, in the manner I have indicated with the Task Questions; however, be careful not to lose the flow of the story. For the bracketed Task Questions, only take a few thoughts from the children before moving on. These quick questions help the class comprehend a story that may, otherwise, be confusing because of the lack of pronouns or proper names. You may want to avoid telling them the title of the story, providing yourself with a good comprehension Task Question for the class while you read it (see below):

(Pre-story) Task Question: What do you think the title of the story is? (If using this TQ then you should return to it once the story has been finished before you embark on any other activities or questions.)

This story is told in the first person, which offers an interesting challenge for a storyteller.

The story

'I can't find it!' said Daddy as he came up from looking in the basement, covered in dust. So I decided to look for it for him.

Task Question 1: Will whoever's telling the story be able to find it?

First of all I looked under the bed and there were three things there. I knew it wasn't the umbrella or the brush, but the third thing was something I didn't know, so I thought that that must *be it.*

Task Question 2: Is the speaker right, must that be it?

'That's not it,' Daddy said when I showed him. He was still looking for it. 'So, what is this *then, Daddy?' I asked.*

'Just a… thing!' he said, not really looking. 'Oh, a Thing. *Not a* This *or a* That? Right,' *I said and went to put the* Thing *back. I had always wondered what a* Thing *was.*

Task Question 3: What is a thing? (This TQ makes a good, longer enquiry; possibly the central enquiry to this session.)

Nested Questions:
- Is a thing something you don't know or can it be something you do know?
- Is a person a thing? A chair?
- Is an object a thing?
- Is a thing the same as an it?
- What does 'thing' mean?
- Can you name something that isn't a thing? (Let them make suggestions first, then test them with the group: 'Is X something that isn't a thing?') How about:
  - Nothing?
  - A fictional character?
  - A feeling?
  - A ghost?
  - How about something that only *might* be there?

Mm, *I thought, where could it be? Then I remembered that Daddy had been looking in the basement first, so I thought that maybe that's where it was meant to be.*

I went down into the dark basement…

I didn't have to look for long, though. Silly Daddy! There it was, trying to hide in the corner. It was far too strangely shaped to be able to hide easily.

'You must be It!' I said.

I think It heard me and I think It looked at me and I think It was a little bit afraid. 'You don't have to be frightened,' I said to It. Then I gave It some of my chocolate. It liked chocolate. Of course It did, everything likes chocolate.

I had never seen anything like It before. Maybe that's why It lived in the basement, so that no one would see It. It's too difficult to describe so I won't. I couldn't decide if It looked right or if It looked wrong. When you don't know what It is, it's difficult to say.

After It had eaten all of my chocolate, It let me get close enough to stroke It. We became friends.

Then I remembered I had been looking for It for my daddy. 'Come on,' I said, 'Let's go and find Daddy.' It let me carry It upstairs.

Task Question 4: What do you think the speaker's Daddy will say or do? Do you think that It was what he was looking for?

When I took It to my daddy, he looked really shocked when I had found what he couldn't.

'You found It!' he shouted with delight.

When he took It from me, he cradled It gently. I said, 'Daddy, why haven't you told me about It before?'

'Erm, erm, I don't know,' he said.

'It's my new best friend,' I said.

'Well, it's out in the open now,' said Daddy. I was pleased I had found It for him.

Now It lives with us. It's one of the family.

Oh, and I've looked every day in the

basement for a Thing and a This and a That but they obviously don't live in the basement. I'll look in the attic next. I've heard some noises up there...

Task Question 5: What is It?

Nested Questions:
- What does the word 'it' mean? Is the word 'it' the same as 'thing'?
- Is It real?
- Can you list the things you know about It from the story?
- What does It look like? Can you draw It?
- Why does 'It' suddenly assume a capital letter half way through the story?
- What would a Thing or a This or a That look like? Can you draw them?
- What does the word 'it' usually describe? What does 'it' describe in this story?
- What might it be? Can a story be about something it only *might* be?
- If it was true that It turned out to be something, does that mean that the speaker was right when he or she thought that It was something but before he or she had found it?
- Is 'It' a name?
- Is there any reason to suppose the speaker a boy or a girl?
- *TX (see page 7) pre-language:* Imagine a time before anybody had any language. What are things without language?
- *Task:* Choose an object. Then get someone to walk into the room and try to communicate something about the object without using any words.

Il Duomo

This session requires some props: you will need an egg and a table on which to balance it. If you are feeling brave, and confident, you could even demonstrate Brunelleschi's solution in front of the class (see below). If so, you may want to practise doing this at home so that you get an idea of the amount of pressure required to crack the egg without it falling apart. I hope you like to eat eggs.

The story is an example of what is known as a *tall tale* (see 'Types of story' on page 5): a tall tale has some basis in historical fact, and involves real people, a real place and a real problem. However, the story, as told, is probably not true in its details. So, it is an *exaggeration*. But, as they say, never let the truth get in the way of a good story; and this is a great story.

The story

In the city of Florence, in Italy, there is a cathedral that was built between 1296 and 1496 [You could ask the class the following question: how long did it take to build?] *and, at that time, it was the largest and most impressive building in all of Europe. It is called the* Basilica di Santa Maria Del Fiore *and is known ordinarily as Il Duomo, which means 'The Dome'. This is because it has a huge dome roof that covers the cathedral like the top of a huge egg. It was not always* known as Il Duomo because the cathedral didn't always have a dome. Once the main structure had been finished in 1418 it was nearly another hundred years before the roof was finally completed. They had tried to build one many times but the structure was so big that it kept falling down; the roof was just too heavy.

For years, people inside the cathedral were at the mercy of the weather and although Italy is known for its good weather it still rains; and when it rains, it rains hard. Italian cities are also famous for their piccione, or pigeons. As well as the rain, the people inside the cathedral were at the mercy of the pigeons too!

Their roofless cathedral was such an embarrassment for the Florentines that it was decided something had to be done: a roof must be built. So it was declared that a competition was to be held. All engineers and architects were invited to submit their plans for building a roof, and a panel of officials would judge all the plans and announce a winner. The winner would then be offered the job to build the roof of the most impressive building in all of Europe; a great honour indeed!

Many illustrious engineers and architects of the day came forward to submit their ideas. One after the other, the panel of judges heard and saw their plans. Towards the end of the day, an artist / architect / sculptor / engineer called Filippo Brunelleschi stood before the panel.

'Okay, show us your plans,' said one of the judges.

Brunelleschi stood motionless.

'Well, are you going to submit your plans or not?' said another, impatiently. They had been doing this all day.

Eventually the architect said, 'I find myself in a predicament: you see, my idea is, principally, very simple and if I share it with you today it is in danger of being stolen; but if I do not tell you my idea then you have nothing to judge and so cannot consider me for the competition.'

'It is indeed a predicament,' said one of the judges, 'but you'll have to take the risk if you want to be considered as a candidate.'

'I have devised a compromise that will allow me to be considered but without giving away my idea,' said the architect, 'Instead of submitting my plans I would like to set you all a task.'

The judges were visibly annoyed by this as it was he that was supposed to be tested, not them, but before they could object Brunelleschi had taken out of his pocket an egg. He held it up before them mysteriously. The sheer absurdity of this silenced the judges and they all leaned in to listen.

'My task is for you to make this egg stand up vertically on the table in front of you without the aid of any implements.' He placed the egg on the table before them and then he said, 'There you are. Go!'

Straight away, the judges set to work like eager school children, so compelling was the task Brunelleschi had set them.

> **Task Question:** Imagine you are one of the judges. How will you complete the task Brunelleschi has set you? (Use the props to attempt this task but remember: *no implements are allowed!*)

Some simply tried, very carefully, to balance the egg while four others blew on it from all sides to try to hold it in one place. Just the sight of these important judges blowing on the egg caused Brunelleschi to chuckle to himself (though he did so silently). Eventually, one of them declared: 'It can't be done! It is impossible!' thereby bringing their attempts to a close.

Without pausing, Brunelleschi walked up to the judges' table and picked up the egg and with a short, quick movement he cracked the base of it on the table so that it stood upright. He then let go and stood back; the egg still remained vertical. The judges looked on in amazement, dumbfounded by the simplicity of his solution.

'Anyone could have done that!' said one of the judges.

'But you didn't; I did.' retorted Brunelleschi.

It is said that on the strength of this demonstration Brunelleschi was offered the job to roof the Basilica. It covers the cathedral to this day and is visited by many thousands of people every year.

The technique, and a (possibly messy) demonstration

Actually, Brunelleschi did not invent the technique he was to use; he merely recovered a technique that had been used by the Romans but that had been forgotten. It was based on the principle of the *arch*. The arch is a structure that is self-supporting so that, once the arch is all in place, no extraneous support is needed. You may have wondered what eggs have to do with the dome. Well, interestingly, an egg's structure is based on the same principles as that of the arch. Just try cracking an egg between your thumb and forefinger by applying pressure on the top and bottom of the egg only (for this to work, it must be an egg without any hairline cracks). This strength protects the egg when it falls from the chicken to the ground. Next, try breaking the egg by holding it in your fist like a cricket ball and squeezing with consistently-spread pressure. If the egg is not already cracked or flawed it will be much more difficult to break than you may think.

Eggs have also evolved the shape they have in order not to roll away from the nest. Check out the unusual shape of an auk's egg, which is laid on bare cliff-face rock, not in a nest; its shape helps it stay on the rock and prevents it from rolling off the cliff and into the sea.

Extension activity: arches

Using polystyrene blocks, are you able to demonstrate how the principle of the arch works as opposed to the weaker rectangular structure that most doors use, for instance? *Hint:* Find out about the 'keystone'.

Research

Having heard the very engaging story of *Il Duomo* set the class the task of researching the history of the building of the dome, and Brunelleschi's role in its completion.

Task Question: How much of the story is true?

Extension activity: an enquiry about flight

The Wright Brothers are said to have been the first men to have achieved artificial human flight in 1903. Leonardo da Vinci, some 400 years earlier, had made many designs for a flying machine, which it is believed he never tested. A Channel 4/PBS programme called *Leonardo's Dream Machines* (2005) tested his flying machine designs. The hang-glider has fared best of all in tests.

Task Question: If Leonardo da Vinci did indeed make a flying machine design that worked, would it have been the Wright brothers or da Vinci who had invented flight?

Nested Questions:
- Could it be said that the writer of a story, such as the story of Daedalus and Icarus, was the inventor of flight? If not, why not? (What's the earliest story of non-magical, artificial, man-made flight that you can find?)
- Could it be said that birds invented flight? If not, why not?
- What is it to 'invent' something?
- What is the difference between invention and discovery?
- Was flight *invented* or *discovered* when humans managed to achieve artificial human flight?

Urban myths

Closely related to the tall tale is the 'urban myth' or legend. From the point of view of thinking, urban myths and legends offer a departure point for thinking about knowledge and how we come to know things, though very few individual urban myths offer much to think about in themselves. Jan Harold Brunvand, author of *Too Good To Be True: The Colossal Book of Urban Legends* (2001), describes urban legends as 'true stories that are too good to be true.' He goes on to say 'These popular fables describe presumably real (though odd) events that happened to a friend of a friend'. In the world of urban myths the 'friend of a friend' has been reduced to the comical acronym 'F.O.A.F' or just 'FOAF'.

He claims that what distinguishes genuine urban myths is that their tellers *believe* them to be real and therein lies their power. As stories they are often not particularly good but with the virtue of being true they become fascinating in an 'Oh my God!' kind of way. By 'too good to be true' Brunvand means that they are too 'polished, balanced, focused, and neat'; there are no loose ends or extraneous details. This, in itself, raises some interesting issues to think about, for instance, in relation to certain kinds of account such as conspiracy theories – themselves often a form of urban myth.

Urban myths also belong to the oral tradition in that they are told and retold by ordinary people. For this reason they undergo myriad variations as in the game 'Chinese Whispers', while holding onto a central, recognisable, narrative heart. Another characteristic feature of an urban myth is that it is *unsourceable* – this is in the nature of the FOAF. So, if you were to hear an urban myth and the teller told you that this 'actually happened to a friend of a friend' then – if it is a genuine urban myth as opposed to a true 'true story' – no matter how much you try, you would never be able to find 'the friend' to whom the event was said to have occurred or to have been witnessed by.

The Magician's Tricks stories

These two original stories were written after an introductory lecture on Arabic philosophy was very kindly delivered to members of The Philosophy Foundation by Professor Peter Adamson (at the time, of King's College, London). *Honest Sa'id* was inspired by a not-as-well-known-as-it-should-be thought-experiment known as 'the flying (or *falling*) man' that has come to us from the philosopher Ibn Sine, anglicised to Avicenna (see bibliography Avicenna, Twelfth Century).

The question he wished to ask using the thought-experiment was: *what would – or could – we know or think if we had no sensory experience?*

Avicenna used this thought-experiment to attempt to demonstrate that the mind / soul is separate from the body. His thought-experiment and his project will be familiar to anyone acquainted with the ideas of Descartes (1641). However, Avicenna's precedes Descartes' by some 500 years. *The Fire-Stick* was inspired by the philosophy of Al Ghazali (see bibliography Al Ghazali, Eleventh Century) who argued, similarly to the later – and more well-known – British philosopher David Hume (1739, 1748), that we cannot identify a necessary connection between events and those events they are said to be the cause of.

Honest Sa'id

Starting age: ten years

Themes:
- Senses
- Knowledge
- Thinking
- Inference
- Inductive knowledge

Before beginning *Honest Sa'id* it is a good idea to ask the class what the five senses are and whether they can list them. It is sometimes thought that a sixth sense, which Avicenna had overlooked, is *proprioception* (relative position), and possibly a seventh, *interoception* (awareness of such things as pain, hunger and the movement of internal organs). Be on the lookout, in an enquiry, for ideas that resemble these. Introduce them with the terms given above, if necessary, rather than trying to simply fit them into the usual five senses. Task Questions 5 and 6 are the main enquiry questions so don't spend too long on the others.

The story

Sa'id was 12 years old and very honest. He was so honest he was incapable of telling a lie. Sa'id worked as a servant for his uncle Naseem who was a magician. Naseem was very clever but he had a vice that he could not give up: he was a gambler. Naseem's wife, Heba, who was always worried about Naseem spending the money they needed to live on, made Sa'id promise to keep an eye on Naseem for her, and to tell her when he gambled. Sa'id promised that he would try to keep an eye out.

Shortly afterwards, Naseem and Sa'id were walking home when they passed a house. Naseem stopped them and tied up their donkeys and told Sa'id to wait outside while he went in. He said he was going, 'to conduct some business'.

That night Naseem was in trouble with his wife for having been gambling.

Task Question 1: How do you think she knew?

The next day Naseem went back to Sa'id and said, 'Did you tell Heba that I was gambling the other day?'

Sa'id could not lie. 'I did. I saw through the window with my own eyes, Uncle.'

When he heard this Naseem was angry with Sa'id so he cast a spell that caused Sa'id to lose his sight. 'If he can no longer see,' thought Naseem, 'I will be able to gamble without getting caught.'

The next day they passed the same gambling house and Naseem went inside to gamble, confident that Sa'id would not know this time.

That night Naseem was told off again by Heba!

> **Task Question 2:** How do you think Heba knew this time?

When he found Sa'id the next morning he said again, 'How did you know that I was gambling?'

'I could hear you through the window, Uncle,' said Sa'id.

This time Naseem cast a spell that caused Sa'id to lose his hearing.

The next day they passed the gambling house again and Naseem entered once more.

And that night Heba told him off again!

> **Task Question 3:** How do you think she knew this time?

'How did you know I was gambling again?' he asked Sa'id again. But, of course, Sa'id could not hear him without his ears so Naseem poked him in the back. Sa'id knew exactly why he had been poked, so he told him:

'When I was getting your clothes ready in the morning I found your money pouch among your clothes and I could feel that it had more than halved in weight, so I knew that you had been gambling again, and because I promised Heba, I had to tell her.'

This time the spell removed his sense of touch.

Naseem was now much more relaxed. Without his sight, hearing or touch surely Sa'id would not be able to know if he had been gambling.

But that night he was told off again, and this time Heba shouted at him louder than before.

'HOW DID YOU KNOW?' He screamed at Sa'id the following morning though he knew that the boy couldn't hear him. Then Naseem poked him again

so that Sa'id would know that he was angry. But Sa'id couldn't feel anything either, so he didn't know that Naseem was angry. Sa'id just sat there sniffing the air, as that was almost all he could do. This gave Naseem a clue: he found the clothes he had been wearing the night before while gambling and he sniffed them. They smelled of tobacco and coffee: the aromas of the gambling house, and he realised that Sa'id had known because of the smell of his clothes.

Naseem then cast a spell to remove Sa'id's sense of smell. Then he remembered that he still had his sense of taste so he cast one more spell to remove his tongue too, just in case! 'Without his tongue Sa'id wouldn't be able to tell Heba anything anyway,' thought Naseem.

'I'm free at last!' he shouted out loud, though Sa'id couldn't hear that either.

The next day he went gambling again confident that Sa'id, without any of his senses, could not find out that he'd been gambling. He could finally relax and gamble without fear of being told off.

That night he got the worst telling off ever!

'HOW DID YOU KNOW AND HOW DID YOU TELL HER?' he screamed at Sa'id, but Sa'id had no idea that Naseem was even there because he could neither feel, smell, hear, see nor taste. Naseem was furious. But he was also frustrated because he had no idea how Sa'id had known and how he had managed to tell Heba. Eventually, it was too much for Naseem so he cast one last spell to return Sa'id's senses to him. Then he demanded that Sa'id tell him how he had known and how he had been able to tell Heba. But Sa'id was no fool, and when he realised that he had his senses back, he sprung to his feet and ran away before Naseem had a chance to cast any more spells. So, Naseem never got to find out how Sa'id had known that he was still gambling.

How do you think he knew?

Task Question 4: How do you think he knew that Naseem was still gambling?

Task Question 5: If someone had, like Sa'id, lost all his or her senses, would he or she know anything at all? If so, what?

Nested Questions:
- Is the brain like a sense organ?
- What can your brain know without any senses?
- What would you know if your memory was removed too?

Sa'id didn't know. But Heba did.

Heba had known because Naseem had been gambling every night before, so Heba thought that it stood to reason that he would gamble every night to come. Heba had simply come to believe that Naseem would gamble every night, and so she reasoned that he had been gambling last night too...

...And she was right, he had.

---

1 Heba believed that Naseem was gambling every night.
2 It was true that Naseem was gambling every night.
3 She believed it because he had gambled every night before and so reasoned that he would gamble every night in the future.

Task Question 6: Do you think Heba did know that Naseem had been gambling?

Nested Questions:
- Is Heba right to think that he will gamble every night in the future because he has gambled every night in the past?
- Can you predict the future from what has happened in the past?
- The sun has risen every day in the past, so does that mean that you know it will rise every day in the future?

This last section is based on a philosophical problem of knowledge known as 'the problem of induction'. In other words, the problem of what we can say about future events based on the evidence of past events. The most famous example of which is Hume's idea (1748) that though one has witnessed the sun rising every day in the past one cannot say with certainty that it will continue to rise every day in the future (and, presumably, one day it will not). The argument (steps 1–3) formulates the problem in the standard 'justified (3)-true (2)-belief (1)' form.

The Fire-Stick!

> **Starting age:** ten years
>
> **Themes:**
> - Magic
> - Science
> - God
> - Causes
> - Over-determination
> - Explanation

The story

Avi was a magician and he had an apprentice called Ahmet. Ahmet was learning how to be a magician but he didn't like how the magicians did everything with magic. They did the washing up with magic, they tidied up with magic and they got dressed with magic. Ahmet thought that magicians were lazy.

He decided that he was going to create a magic show with a difference: it would be a magic show with no magic. But for this he would need a different kind of teacher. He went to see a scientist. The scientist had been working on a new invention. It was a small stick that had been dipped in sulphur so that there was a small ball of sulphur on one end. Sulphur is a substance that burns well.

The scientist had also made a wooden box that had a rough, sandy side to it. He had made it by gluing sand to the side of the box. Inside the box he placed the sulphur-sticks.

Task Question 1: Can you work out what the 'fire-stick' is?

He showed Ahmet how it worked:

'Watch,' he said, 'you take out the stick and strike it against the side of the box like this.' He struck the sulphur-end of the stick against the sandy side. Suddenly a flame lit up. Ahmet jumped out of his skin, he was so alarmed. The flame burned fiercely for a moment before dying down and eventually going out.

'I said no magic!' exclaimed Ahmet.

Task Question 2: Is it magic?

Nested Questions:
- What is magic?
- What is science?
- What is the difference between the two?

'It's not magic,' assured the scientist. 'Let me explain how it works…' and he proceeded to explain exactly how the 'fire-stick' worked. Ahmet wasn't sure if he fully understood, but he was at least satisfied that it wasn't magic.

(As the teacher, you may want to take this opportunity to explain – and possibly demonstrate safely – exactly how a match works.)

Ahmet advertised his first magic show and he called it 'The Fire-Stick – The Magic Show Without Magic!' Many people heard about the strange trick that he was going to perform but the strangest thing, they all thought, was that it would be done without magic. 'It can't be done!' some of them said. Avi also heard about it and he was worried that Ahmet would make a fool of himself. 'No one can make fire just come out of a stick without magic, not without rubbing it for a really long time,' thought Avi. And then he came up with another of his plans. To save Ahmet embarrassment he decided that he would hide at the side of the stage, so that Ahmet wouldn't know he was there. Then, just at the moment that

Ahmet struck the stick on the side of the box, he would cast a 'fire-spell' to make sure that it lit.

And that is exactly what he did. To begin with, Ahmet performed some very impressive card tricks and some tricks where he seemed to be able to read people's minds, and then he ended the show with 'the amazing fire-stick trick'. The audience was amazed. How did he do it? Some people said that it was a hoax and that really he had used some magic without anyone noticing.

'But it wasn't magic!' insisted Ahmet to the doubters. He began to explain to his audience exactly how the tricks worked.

'It was magic really,' Avi thought to himself, but he didn't say anything out loud.

Summary 1 (read this out to the class before asking the Task Question):
Ahmet was convinced that *he* was the cause of the fire-stick lighting because he knew that if he struck the fire-stick it would light. Avi, however, believed that it was *he* that was the cause of the fire-stick lighting as he had cast a fire-spell at the very moment that Ahmet had struck it.

Task Question 3: So, who was the cause of the fire-stick lighting, Ahmet or Avi?

And then the Mullah stepped out from within the audience.

'You are right. It wasn't magic,' said the Mullah, the holy man, who, having heard so much about it, had attended the show. 'It was a miracle,' *he said. 'It was a miracle because everything is a miracle. Everything that happens, happens for one reason only: and that is that God makes it happen.' He looked at Avi. 'When you cast a spell, God makes it happen.' Then he looked at Ahmet. 'And if you kick a stone, God makes the stone move. He could make the stone turn into a flower when you kicked it if he wanted!'*

'So, why doesn't he?' asked Ahmet. 'Why doesn't something different happen every time I kick a stone?'

'Because,' replied the Mullah, 'God doesn't joke around like you silly magicians. He wants to make life easier for us all so he makes the same thing happen every time we do something. But he doesn't have to. And he doesn't always. When God makes something different happen it is called a miracle.'

Summary 2:

Ahmet was convinced that *he* was the cause of the fire-stick lighting because he knew that if he struck the fire-stick it would light. Avi, however, believed that *he* was the cause of the fire-stick lighting as he had cast a fire-spell at the very moment that Ahmet had struck it. And the Mullah believed that *God* was the cause of the fire-stick lighting as God was busy making everything happen.

Task Question 4: So, who was the cause of the fire-stick lighting, Ahmet, Avi or God?

Nested Questions:
- What is the difference between science and religious explanations for why things happen?
- Are there any similarities between science and religious explanations?
- What is a miracle?
- Is a miracle the same as magic?
- Could they all be right?
- Could the cause of the match lighting have been the author of the story. And, if so, could the author make anything happen and would that then make it a miracle?
- TX (see page 7) Magic: Imagine a world in which magic is normal? (Use this for the basis of a *What if?* story-writing activity).

Extension activity: a magic show!

To add a little spice and fun to this session you could perform your own 'magic show' for the class. When I do this I do three 'tricks', but carefully chosen to be very different kinds of trick. All the tricks referred to here are easily available online or in magic books. Alternatively, some suitable tricks can be found in the lesson plan *Things Are Not Always What They Seem*, available for download from The Philosophy Foundation website (in the free members section: www.philosophy-foundation.org). For your magic show you will need:

1 A conventional magic trick, such as the ring that 'defies gravity' by 'moving' up an inclined elastic band. Any trick of this kind will do. *Hint:* make sure you practise the trick so that you can perform it confidently and remember: do not reveal how the trick works (magicians never reveal their secrets!) as this will provide the class with a strong motivation to find out and disseminate to each other.

2 An illusion, such as 'the magic finger' that is produced by holding up your index fingers before your eyes, but focusing your eyes on the wall behind. Again, any illusion will work.

3 Something incredible but not a trick, such as The Mobius Strip demonstration or 'shrinking coin' trick where the two-pence piece is slipped through a hole in a piece of paper only the size of a one pence piece (see 'Things are not always what they seem' above).

Task Question: Which of these tricks, if any, is magic? Exactly why is it, or is it not, magic?

Nested Questions:
- What makes something magic?
- Is something magic if it is unbelievable?
- Is something magic if you don't know how it happens?
- Is something magic if you want to believe that it is magic?
- Is a trick magic if performed by a magician?
- Is an illusion magic?

Stories in verse

Stories in verse often require the audience to work harder than they would with a prose narrative because of certain features of form and style (words limited within stanza; strict rhythm and / or rhyme) so connections between stanzas are not always spelled out, as they might be in a prose story. For this reason there may be greater rewards but it is also – for the same reason – important for the teacher/facilitator to take certain steps to maximise the class's capability to access narrative in verse.

A story in verse is the ultimate test of the storyteller's art. If a class of children is able to understand the narrative of a story in verse through your telling, then you may feel confident that your telling is of a high standard. This section of the book, therefore, is for the more advanced storyteller. It is also a good way to self-assess. All of the poems included in this book have been tested with classes and so have proved accessible, which means that it's now down to you to maximise their accessibility.

Unfamiliar words

When approaching a poem for its poetry (language, metaphor, conceit etc.) then, and especially if there are only a few new words or phrases, it is preferable to read the poem first and approach new words and phrases in the context of the poem itself. However, if you are using a poem primarily for its narrative content, I would suggest learning the new words before reading or telling the poem. I have included an *Unfamiliar words* list before each poem to help prepare for this. The procedure I use is as follows:

1 First, write up the unfamiliar words list on the board and ask if there is anyone who thinks they already know any of the words. Write up meanings of the words they know first. *Note:* I keep the meanings simple and relevant (e.g. '*fortune*, for our purposes today, means *luck*'). As long as you have the meaning that allows the children to follow the story, then that should be

sufficient and will not clutter their minds. But certainly don't dismiss other correct suggestions made by the children.

2 With any words they don't know, provide a context and then ask if anyone would like to have a go at inferring or guessing what they think the word means (e.g. If the word is 'cease', the context could be: 'Then the teacher said, "Could you please *cease* your chattering?"') With each context, and if appropriate, try to perform an action to accompany the sentence, this will be helpful for recall. Tone of voice may help too. (See 'Vocabulary' on page 50 for more on this.)

3 (Optional) Once all the words have meanings, ask them to look at them and to try to remember as many as possible, then after 30 seconds or so, rub them off / delete them. Randomly select members of the class to recall a word, if they get stuck then, first of all, repeat the context (with the action if there is one), and if they are still stuck ask, 'can you remember any of them?' Carry on until all the words have been recalled and are written up again.

Perform the poem

Once the unfamiliar words have been made familiar, you are ready to recite or read your poem.

How well the children follow the poem's story will depend very much on how well you read or recite your poem, once the vocabulary is in place. If your memory is good then reciting the poem is the best way, as it frees up your hands, eyes and body for gestures, eye contact and movement (see 'Sheherazad's handbook' on page 20). These all help to support the class's understanding because the communication is direct and immediate.

If, as is more likely, you choose to read the poem, then practise reading it so that you clearly convey the meaning and dramatic structure of the poem / narrative. (See 'Speaking and lifting from the page' on page 28.)

Piecing together

Ask the class to say what they think happens in the story and / or to ask questions about anything that is unclear or that they don't understand. Wherever possible, enlist the class to answer questions rather than do it yourself. Read or recite, again, any lines or sections that would help them answer their questions if they struggle to do so.

Repeat your performance

Once they have had a good attempt to work through the poem repeat your performance. Having worked through it, they will find the second reading much more comprehensible. Your actions and gestures will help here too.

Going deeper

Once their comprehension is in place you are in a position to move to the enquiry part of the lesson.

- *Emergent Enquiry*: Sometimes a question or discussion emerges from the comprehension part of the exercise. For instance, one boy said, after hearing *The Luckiest Man In the World* (see page 177), 'You can't create your own luck'. This is what I call an emergent question (see Emergent Questions and Enquiries on page 59). Either reframe it as a question ('Can you create your own luck?') and put it to the class, or simply put it to the class as said, (Teacher: 'Abdul said "You can't create your own luck"; what do you [the class] think about that?').
- *Task Question*: If using this book, you could turn to the task questions after the poem. If you find a more appropriate question among the nested questions then use that.
- *The Concept Box*: Alternatively, you could use the strategy described on page 77; if you have already done the comprehension part above, then use only the *concept fishing* and *concept funnelling* parts of the Concept Box procedure.

(See 'Stories in verse' on page 166 and Appendix 1 'Quick view steps' on page 207).

The Magic Crown

Starting age: seven years

Themes:
- Power
- Rulership
- Rules and laws
- The legitimacy of rulership
- Choices

This is a long poem for young children but if read in three sections, with questions and an enquiry at the end of each, it becomes perfectly digestible. Despite its having enjambment and a few unfamiliar words I have found that, with the correct delivery, children as young as seven have been able to access the thought-experiment the poem puts to them. If you are uncomfortable exploring the legitimacy of monarchy with very young children, then the poem still sounds complete with the last stanza omitted. It's nice to read this with a prop – a crown if you can find or make one (see 'Minimal prop principle' on page 47).

Unfamiliar words:

These are the words that are likely to lie in the way of your class's understanding of the narrative in the poem. (See 'Unfamiliar words' at the beginning of this section on page 166 for more on this part of the process.)

- citizen
- to *happen* upon
- pose
- don
- wrestle
- opt
- enact
- to *pass* rules.

The story

You live in a land somewhat different from ours
This land has a crown with magical powers
The crown looks – if you look – like an ordinary one
But is far from ordinary when placed upon
The head of a citizen, be it boy or girl,
Because any head under it rules the whole world!

One day you happen upon this magic crown
And when you see it, you scratch your chin,
Strike a thoughtful pose, and frown.
You frown because now you've got to decide
Whether you'll don it or just continue to glide
Right past so someone else has to wrestle instead
With whether or not they'll place this weight on their head.

Task Question 1: If you found it, would you put the magic crown on?

Nested Questions:
- Would you be able to do what you want?
- Are there any responsibilities involved in ruling?
- Do you (the ruler) decide whether there are any responsibilities or not? If not, then who does?
- Would it be fun or hard work?

Let's now imagine that you opt for the crown
To sit on your head instead of the ground.
The first thing our new queen or king must enact
Are some rules that the rest of the world respect.
What rules would you pass that all must obey?
Write a list! So that everyone knows what they say.

> **Task Question 2:** If you were to 'don it' (put it on) what rules or laws would you enact?
>
> Nested Questions:
> - What rules would be good rules?
> - What would *make* them good rules?
> - Are there any rules that you *must* or *must not* have?
> - Are there any rules that the ruler has to follow?
> - Who or what rules the ruler?

(Optional section, see above.)

Is it right that a ruler be picked like this?
If not, then just what do you suggest?
Are there rules that rule which ruler should rule?
Or do rulers decide for themselves just who'll
Be the Queen – or King, for that matter – over us?
Would it be better if nobody does?

> **Task Question 3:** How should a ruler be selected?
>
> Nested Questions:
> - Is there a fair way to select a ruler?
> - Should someone be more important than everyone else?
> - Is the ruler more important than everyone else?
> - Should there be no ruler?
> - Maybe everyone should rule. What do you think?
> - What would make a good ruler?
> - Should there be rules to protect the people from the ruler?

The Square That Didn't Fit In

Starting age: nine years

Themes:
- Difference
- Alienation
- Misunderstandings
- Shapes
- *Squircles* (an imaginary shape which is a combination of a square and a circle. Word invented by nine-year-old Élody.)

This story can be used for a number of contrasting issues for thinking. It allows for a discussion on the nature of logical possibility in the notion of 'round squares' or, more simply, it can be used to explore the features of a square and / or a circle. It also touches upon personal identity (such as discussions around gender) in that it allows for a discussion about what it is that makes a person who he or she is.

Unfamiliar words:
- equality
- malicious
- devour.

The story

'I don't want to be a square anymore!'
Said the square that didn't fit in
'I feel too round and circular
And I roll – at least when dreaming.

'I was born with a sense of equality
But don't want to be treated the same
Because I have a different quality,'
Said the square that didn't fit in

'I may look like a square to you
But I'm a circle on the inside.

Were lines to cross my heart
They would measure the same distance wide,'

Said the square that didn't fit in.

One day a shape-eating monster
Arrived with a square-shaped mouth
Each day it would eat a square
And then fly back off to the south.

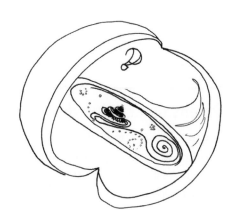

But our square that didn't fit in
Had no reasons left to live
So he took himself to the monster,
His life to the monster he'd give

The monster took one look at the square
And said, 'Square, you look delicious!'
He'd never seen such a tasty looking square
'And you,' said the square, 'look malicious.

'But I'm not a square,' explained the square,
'I'm really a circle, you see.'
'What!' said the monster, 'You mean: you're not a square?
'Oh, my mistake, I am sorry!'

Then the monster flew off, embarrassed,
Looking for squares to devour
Thinking that circles are squares
It reached Circle-Land in less than an hour.

But the circles, of course, didn't fit
Into its square-shaped mouth
So the monster, by now starving hungry,
Flew off back down to the south.

From that day on the squares agreed
They'd regard the square a 'circle'
'Oh thank you, my friends! For that
I will be eternally grateful,'

Said the square that didn't fit in.

Task Question 1: Can a square be a circle?

Nested Questions:
- What is a square?
- What is a circle?
- Can these two ideas (the idea of a square and the idea of a circle) go together?

Extension activity: drawing a round square

Set the class the task of drawing a *round square*. Allow them to try, on a small whiteboard or piece of paper, and then get them to share their attempts with the rest of the class. With each attempt that's shown ask the class: 'Have they succeeded in drawing a round square?' and then *open it up* (see 'Iffing, anchoring and opening up' on page 74) with 'Why?' or 'Then how would you do it?'

Nested Questions:

- Is it possible to draw a round square?
- Could you succeed by inventing a new shape called a 'Squircle' – a combination of a square and a circle? Would it be a round square?
- Are all things possible, or are some things impossible?
- Does impossible mean that you can never do it?
- Exactly what does 'square' mean? Exactly what does 'round' mean? (Look them up.)
- Do the meanings help you answer the question, *Is it possible to draw a round square?*

Task Question 2: What did the square mean when it said 'I may look like a square... but I'm a circle on the inside'?

Nested Questions:
- What does it mean to say that you are one thing on the outside but another on the inside?
- Can a dog be a cat on the inside (or a cat a dog)? (See the story *The Cat That Barked* on page 112.)
- (Optional, age-appropriate question) Can a girl be a boy on the inside (or a boy a girl)?

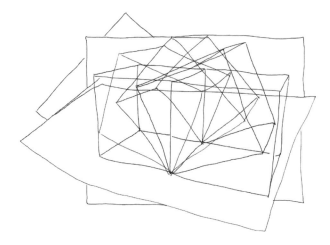

Extension activity: stories and poetry

Here is another (the original) version of *The Square That Didn't Fit In* but this time written as a *poem* instead of a *story in verse*.

Unfamiliar words:
- declare
- rigid
- congregate
- tessellate.

The Square That Circled

The story

I've got four sides,
I'm four-corners-wide,
Equally spaced apart.

They say I'm a square
But I have to declare
I'm a circle in my heart.

Squares are too rigid
With no space in between
When they come together to congregate.

I, however,
Don't seem to fit in,
I simply refuse to tessellate.

Task Question: What is the difference between *The Square That Didn't Fit In* and *The Square That Circled*?

Nested Questions:
- Are they both poems?
- Is *The Square That Circled* a story?
- Is *The Square That Didn't Fit In* a poem?
- What is the difference between a story in verse and a poem?

The Luckiest Man in The World

Starting age: ten years

Themes:
- Luck / skill
- Providence
- Fate
- Destiny
- Power

I have *versed* this story, which comes from Herodotus' *Histories* (see bibliography, circa 430 BCE), thought by many to be the first history book by the first historian of Western Europe. There are many versions of 'the returning ring' theme but this is the earliest I know of, told, not as a fiction story but as history.

This story has, what is known as a 'reveal', in the last two words. I have interrupted the rhyme pattern to delay the reveal thereby giving the audience a little extra time to anticipate it: the horror of the reveal all the more *horrorable* for having been anticipated. This is a classic example of a *tale with a twist* (see page 6).

Unfamiliar words:
- fortune
- unfurl
- tyrant
- wrathful
- cease
- hurled
- sought
- mirth.

The story

Polycrates of Samos was the luckiest king in the world
Fortune always favoured him in battles that unfurled;
The wind blew his ships faster,
His enemy's ships off-course;

At times a natural disaster
Would lessen his enemy's force.

Now, Amasis of Egypt was the most fearful king alive,
As Polycrates marched closer he had come to realise
That he would have to ask the king of Samos
To enter an agreement,
Protecting each from the other
And making both a tyrant.

Polycrates and Amasis were the most powerful kings there were,
But no instance of misfortune ever once occurred.
Amasis was fearful
So he complained to Polycrates,
Fearing the gods wrathful
If his fortune did not cease.

A beautiful, jewelled ring was the most valuable thing in the world
To Polycrates, who stood upon a cliff from which he hurled
The ring into the raging tide
Which carried it out to sea
Proving to the gods on high
He could find misery.

Amasis and Polycrates were the happiest men on Earth
Free of his ring and the wrath of the gods they sought to find some mirth;
The cooks prepared a swordfish,
The biggest ever seen!
But when they sliced it open
Inside they found –
– To the horror of the tyrants –
Inside they found…
The ring.

Note: With the verse version of this story I suggest using the Concept Box technique described on page 77 instead of using the Task Question that follows the story version. (For the prose story version log on to the online resources that accompany this book.)

Hint: You may want to try both versions with different (or the same) classes to compare and contrast presenting a story in two very different ways: a prose narrative and a verse-story. Make a note of the differences, advantages and disadvantages that come with each mode of presentation.

Extension activity: luck

- Play any game that involves an element of luck such as *Pig* (See Fisher's *Games For Thinking,* 1997) to use as a vehicle for discussing instances of good / bad luck and skill.
- *Black!* This is a card game that can produce some astonishing results if played with large numbers of players. To play:
  - Tell the class that the aim of the game is to get a black card.
  - Shuffle a deck of cards.
  - Deal the cards so that each player has one card in front of him or her, placed face down so that they can't see it.
  - Ask everyone to turn their card over simultaneously and to see whether they have a black or a red card – the winners of the round are those that have black cards.
  - Now play a second round, as above. Then a third, a fourth and perhaps a fifth and sixth (when you stop is up to you). After each round see if there is anybody who got a black card successively on each round.

  If there is a good number of players, then, statistically, there should be someone who gets a black card for most, if not all, of the rounds (this usually happens successfully with a class size of 25-30 children). This can seem extraordinary but is simple probability and makes for a good starting point for a discussion. For instance, the aim of the game – to get a black card – is completely arbitrary; it could have been a red card. Some people may have had red every time but they are less likely to have seen this as extraordinary, given that it was not stated to be the aim of the game.

- *The Monty Hall Problem:* Research this famous, but complicated (too complicated for me to explain here, I'm afraid) probability problem. Use it as the starting point of a discussion about probability and luck. Like the Mobius Strip, this is a wonderful example of how something logical and demonstrable goes counter to our common sense, thereby showing the limits of common sense reasoning.

The Arabian Nights and The Sindbad Stories

Starting age: ten years
Themes: see each story

In *The Arabian Nights* one finds early examples (in some cases, I'm sure, the *earliest* examples) of some classic genres not generally thought to have been invented until much later. *The Ebony Horse* gave us science fiction (usually attributed to Mary Shelley's *Frankenstein*, 1818), *The Three Apples* gave us crime fiction (usually attributed to Edgar Allen Poe's *Murders in The Rue Morgue*, 1841) and Sindbad And The Pit (see page 196) prefigures the horror of Edgar Allen Poe (especially his fixation with premature burials in stories such as *The Pit and The Pendulum*, 1842, and *The Cask of Amontillado*, 1846) and the genre of *tales with a twist* (see page 6). I think it's fair to say that I have, ever so slightly, flavoured my own style of writing for the Sindbad stories with a little Poe.

These stories are included in *The Arabian Nights* collection (Lyons, Malcolm and Ursula, 2010) but, together with *Ali Baba and The Forty Thieves* and *Aladdin*, they are thought to have been a later addition. Versions of these stories appear as far afield as India. Not all of Sindbad's adventures have been included here, and, on occasions, I have combined stories. The story of *The Giant Snake* has been woven into *The Valley of The Diamonds* and this was easy enough to do given that the latter story featured snakes. My adaptations are reasonably faithful to the original stories but I have not always returned Sindbad home to Baghdad.

The Two Sindbads

Themes:
- Poverty and hardship
- Justice and fairness
- Inequality
- Wealth and wealth distribution

The story

There was once a man called Sindbad – Sindbad the porter, for he carried other people's belongings on his back for a living. It was trying work and on this particular *day he was feeling* particularly *sorry for himself as he carried a* particularly *heavy load. But then he stopped in his tracks at the sound of music floating down from an overhead window. The window was high up, belonging to a beautiful house that was resplendent and remarkably well-kept.*

Perhaps moved by the beauty of this house or perhaps simply by the sound of the birds singing he fell to his knees and began to pray to Allah, and he spoke of how God made some rich and others poor but how it was not the place of Sindbad to question the ultimate will of God, just that it seemed odd how these differences had come to us though we are all made the same. He made his prayer in song. Not long after he had finished, a boy came down from the splendid house and invited Sindbad in to meet his master.

Task Question: Is it right that some people have so much and others have so little?

Nested Questions:
- Is it right? Is it fair?
- Is *right* the same as *fair*?
- Can it be unfair but still right?
- *TX* (see page 7) *equal money:* If you had the power to make everyone have the same amount of money as each other, overnight, would it be right to do it?
- If you could do *TX equal money, would* you? If you could, should you?
- If you could do *TX equal money* what would happen?
- Does hard work justify inequality?

The boy's master was also named Sindbad and he had heard the song of Sindbad the porter and wished to hear more. When Sindbad the porter had finished reciting more of his song the second Sindbad looked at him and said in a delighted voice, 'I would like to tell you a remarkable tale about how I came about my riches, because it was not without hardship and toil'.

Sindbad the porter sat down, reached for a date and prepared to listen as the second Sindbad began his tale.

The Island

> **Themes:**
> - Knowledge
> - Certainty
> - Accounting for knowledge

The story

Sindbad the sailor said:

'*I was born wealthy in the city of Baghdad and wanted for nothing. I spent my wealth as if it were an endless spring without a thought for the future. But one day the spring ran dry and, almost without noticing, I became poor. Whilst I wondered about what to do I recalled some lines of poetry that advised that no man who does not venture forth will ever gain anything. Nothing will come without effort and risk. So, I resolved to travel on a ship. I sold all my things and raised a reasonable amount of capital, then joined a merchant ship from Basra. It sailed from island to island buying, bartering and selling. Believe it or not, I became wealthy again but no sooner had I become so than I was to lose it all. This is the way of fate, against which we can do nothing.*

'*You see, we arrived on an island that was nothing short of paradise. Every fruit grew on the island and we stayed there for some time. Many of us explored the island while others had fun and played games. But every night we all gathered together around a fire and told each other tales of seafaring and much else besides. Maybe because sailors live such precarious lives, their futures uncertain, one night we got to talking about what we can be sure of. A very philosophical discussion it was too.*

'*"How can we really be sure of anything?" one of our company had said rather curiously.*

'*"Well, I don't know about you, but I'm sure that I'm a sailor and that we have found paradise," said another.*

'*"Maybe. But maybe," replied the first, "this is all a dream. This paradise island does seem too good to be true."*'

This is a good place to stop the story and to ask the class what they think about the sailors' discussion. Write the ideas up like so:

A: What can we be sure of?
B: I'm sure that we have found a paradise island.
A: But how do you know that this isn't all just a dream?
B:

Before reading, or writing up, what the sailors say, for the next part, let the class make their own suggestions and ask them if they can guess what B will say in response to A. (*Note*: this exercise is not just about guessing what the sailors say but also – and mainly – about what the children think, so if they don't guess correctly take a real interest in what they say instead.) Then write up the next part of the dialogue but as a formal argument:

B: If you pinch yourself that proves that you are not dreaming.

A:

Next, ask, first of all, whether they agree with B's argument, followed by what they think A will say in response. Again, try not to make this only a guessing exercise. I have deliberately left out B's reasons for why pinching yourself proves that you are not dreaming. This is because it is for the class to think of reasons. The sort of reasons I've heard classes include are as follows: 'If you pinch yourself and it hurts then you can't be dreaming because you can't feel pain in your dreams'. This, as I'm sure you can imagine, leads to a discussion of whether or not one can feel pain in a dream. I have also heard that 'If you pinch yourself and you don't wake up then you're not dreaming'. When you and / or the class are ready, continue writing up the dialogue had between the two sailors:

A: You could be dreaming that you are pinching yourself.

Follow this with more discussion about who they agree with most: A or B. The entire dialogue should be on the board for the class to see and assess for themselves:

A: What can we be sure of?
B: I'm sure that we have found a paradise island.
A: But how do you know that this isn't all just a dream?
B: If you pinch yourself that proves that you are not dreaming.
A: You could be dreaming that you are pinching yourself.

When you and / or the class are ready continue with the story.

Sindbad the sailor continued:
   "All I have to do," said the second, "is pinch myself to discover if this is nothing but a dream or not." He pinched himself. "See! It's not a dream and I've proved it."

"You could be dreaming that you just pinched yourself," replied the first.

"One thing I'm sure of," said I, "is that the ground is beneath my feet." I was so pleased with myself for having found something I considered to be absolutely certain that I jabbed my knife into the earth to finish my point.

'Just then the earth moved. I got up and went to the beach to see if the ship had felt the surge. I shouted to the ship's captain, who had remained on board. He shouted back in horror for he could see something from the ship we could not.

"Get off that island if you value your lives!" shouted the captain. "For it is not an island but a giant turtle! It has woken up and is looking to dive into the sea again." Sure enough, we looked to see its huge head, craning round to see what was on its back and what had woken it from its ancient slumbers.

'We had no time to gather our things or return to the ship. The creature plunged into the sea's depths having languished long on the surface – long enough to allow forests to spring up on its back, and rivers and lakes to form. We found ourselves bobbing up and down in the open ocean like bottles cast adrift as we watched the ship vanish behind the horizon leaving us to the whim of fate once more.

'And while fate gives, it also takes away.'

Task Question: Sindbad was wrong about the ground beneath his feet. What, if anything, can we know for certain?

Nested Questions:
- What is certainty?
- What is knowledge?
- Can something be known for certain?
- If not, then how certain do we need to be to be able to say that we know something?
- Could we be dreaming right now? How can we tell if we are dreaming or not?
- Is feeling certain the same as being certain?

The Valley of The Diamonds

Themes:
- Solitude
- Laws and rules
- Value
- Wealth
- Despair

The story

'What happened?' asked Sindbad the porter, 'How did you come to be sitting here telling me this tale?'

Sindbad the sailor said:

'Well, fate gave once more. I was eventually picked up by a ship. Shortly after, I was shipwrecked alone on a desolate island with nothing but berries to sustain me. I was found by another merchant ship that passed by my island (for, seeing as no one else shared it with me, I had come to think of the island as my own). On the island I could create my own laws and I needed only do what pleased me. In a way, without the laws of society instructing me what to do, I was happy there. I was free of the demands that others make on us.

'But, as I said, eventually I was found and rescued – if "rescued" is the right word! And, by chance, the ship I had been rescued by had picked up my belongings. Although, it was only due to the goodwill of the captain that I was able to reclaim them, as he believed me when I told him that they were mine. To him I was eternally grateful. Or would have been, if fate had not taken away my wealth once more.

'But before that happened I was returned to Baghdad with my riches and I lived a life of pleasure and happiness as I had before. However, it was as if I had learned nothing from my first voyage, as I continued down the route of intemperance and profligacy. But before long, I got an itch I could not scratch. I longed to be at sea again, even though my first attempt had gone so disastrously wrong.

'But the hankering to travel would not leave me, so I borrowed some more money and bought some more goods for another voyage that I hoped would bring me yet more wealth, solving my financial problems. Maybe it was the longing for adventure that picked up my legs again, or maybe it was just greed, but adventure is what I got, though only through my own foolishness.'

TX solitude: Suppose you were entirely alone and lived without having any other people to have to consider.

Task Question: If you were entirely alone, like Sindbad when on 'his' island (or in *TX Solitude*) would you need to follow any laws?

Nested Questions:
- If not laws, would there be any kind of moral code that you would have to follow or stick to?
- Or could you, like Sindbad supposes, do whatever you wanted?
- Is Sindbad right to suppose that with no one around he is free to do what pleases him?
- To what extent do laws and moral codes depend upon other people?
- Can you think of anything it would be wrong to do even if there were no other people to worry about?
- What about animals? Are there any moral codes regarding animals that we may have to consider?
- What about the environment? Are there any moral codes regarding the environment that we may have to consider?
- What are laws?
- What are laws for?
- What is a moral code?
- What is a moral code for?

'We had moored on another island and a landing party had been sent onto it. A paradise it was, a turtle it was not; not this time. I found my way to a lovely murmuring stream, next to which I sat down and ate some of the food I had taken with me. The stream – perhaps also the wine and the food – lulled me to sleep before long. When I awoke I was horrified to discover that the ship had left without me! I had been completely forgotten. I cursed myself for having been so foolish. Not a week ago I had been enjoying the comforts of my pleasurable life in Baghdad and I had left it all for this. I wept and wailed for my lot, like a child. But being alone, no one saw me.

'When I had pulled myself together I climbed up to a high point from where I was able to survey the island. I thought the island uninhabited but could see a large, curious dome-shaped object in the distance on the side of a mountain. Assuming that nothing like it is made naturally, I concluded that it must be a man-made construct and that if I ventured towards it I might well find civilised assistance. But when I reached the strange object there were no doors or windows into it, its sides perfectly smooth.

'My questions were soon answered as it suddenly went dark as if the sun had been put out. I looked up to see that the sun had been blotted out by a huge bird. I recalled that I had heard tales of these birds – known as a roc – by sailors but I had never thought the tales true. The great bird came to rest on top of the dome, which I now knew to be its egg. After the terror had passed, it dawned on me that this huge bird could be my ticket away from the island, as it was quite unaware of me. I unwound my turban and tied myself to the leg of the roc.

'Sure enough, when the morning came, it took off, taking me with it. The roc did indeed fly away from the island and over the sea for many leagues but I had no idea where it was taking me. All I could do was to pray that it would take me to a civilised land. Eventually it came to rest on the side of a steep mountain. I didn't have much time to act so quickly untied the turban and dropped onto the ground. It was good that I did because no sooner was I on the ground than the bird was off again.

'It swooped and landed on what I thought was a fallen tree trunk a little further down into the valley, but from the struggle that followed I saw that the roc had landed on a giant snake. The bird then took off once more but this time taking the snake with it, disappearing over the mountain ridge, no doubt to return to its island again. Wherever I was, I had been marooned there.

'I looked around to take in my situation. It was clear that I could not go up as the mountainside was virtually sheer and the cliff face ran all the way around, completely enclosing me in this strange valley. I could also see two things, one of which filled me with curiosity and the other, horror: the ground all about this valley glistened as if there were a carpet of glass. But the ground also moved. It was alive with snakes! There were snakes of all sizes: some tiny but many the size of the one I'd seen taken by the roc. And I was trapped!

'The base of the cliff face was dotted with caves all around but I was unable to find shelter there as they were full of snakes, particularly in the day, for many of them hid from the birds of prey that circled the air above the valley. The snakes were active by night. My only refuge was a singular tree that I was able to climb each night in order to sleep – if I managed to sleep at all. When I did manage to catch a wink or two, I dreamt of snakes.

'I had also discovered that the glass carpet I had seen was in fact diamonds that had evidently been formed in the rocks of this valley and had somehow been deposited in and on the ground. They were everywhere. I had never seen such wealth, and though I was probably the richest man in the world, the diamonds were of no use at all to me. I would have given them all for some bread and cheese, a rope and a boat.'

Task Question: In the valley of the diamonds is Sindbad rich?

Nested Questions:
- What makes something valuable?
- What is value?
- *TX* (see page 7) *Health or wealth:* suppose you had to choose between
  A: great wealth but poor health, or
  B: very good health but no wealth.
  If you had to choose, which would you opt for and why?
- What is more important: health or wealth?
- Why are diamonds valuable when Sindbad is in society, but of no value when he is trapped in the valley of the diamonds?
- Is bread, cheese, rope and a boat really more valuable than an endless supply of diamonds?
- *TX Making money:* suppose you were stranded with a group of others on a desert island. After establishing a rudimentary society between you, how would you go about creating money? What would you need to do?
- How does money work?
- How do you think money began?
- What makes money valuable?
- If Sindbad had entered 'the valley of the dollar bills or pound notes', instead of diamonds, would he be rich then?

'On the second night, my sleep was disturbed even more as one of the larger snakes I had seen came hissing around my tree. On the third night, it came up the tree a little and, on the fourth, it ventured even further up. I realised that I could either simply wait until the snake reached me then let it end my wretchedness, or I could act. I have to confess, and though I am not proud to admit it, I did seriously consider letting the snake take me, such was my despair. But, in the end, I decided to endeavour to survive.

'I was able, with the few resources at my disposal, to construct a rudimentary cage that was just big enough to encase me. That very night, the snake came all the way up the tree, coiled itself around my cage and then constricted. My cage was only just able to withhold itself against the snake's constrictions but I was relieved to discover that I had built an adequate protection.'

Teacher's note: if you decide that this discussion is appropriate with your class (depending on age, maturity etc.) then approach it carefully and with sensitivity. It could be used, for instance, to segue into a discussion of the issues surrounding euthanasia, again, if this is appropriate for your class.

Task Question: Was Sindbad right to consider allowing the snake to take him?

Nested Questions:
- Why did Sindbad say that he was not proud to admit it?
- Could it ever be right to die instead of live?
- What is hope?
- When is there hopelessness?
- What do we live for?
- What is life?
- Why is living valuable?

'On the morning of exactly one week since I had been abandoned by the roc, I was awoken by the sound of what I thought was an avalanche. Looking up, I saw something hurtling down the mountainside at great speed. When it finally reached the bottom, it was not too far from me, so I made my way towards the strange object. When I reached it, I discovered that it was a skinned animal; a cow I believe. I followed, with my eye, the trajectory the carcass had made and, at the top of the mountain ridge, I saw some men. The bloody, sticky carcass was coated in diamonds. I realised what it was the men were attempting to do. If I was right, then the best course of action was not a pleasant one.

'After stuffing my pockets and the inside of my shirt with diamonds I quickly lifted the dead animal and climbed underneath, despite the protestations from my nose: the smell was disgusting. I tied myself to it using my turban again and waited. It wasn't long before one of the giant birds that regularly patrolled the sky above the valley spotted the fresh meat, and I was up in the air again.

'Once the bird had begun to fly over the men, they harried it with stones that they fired from a catapult-like device until the bird dropped its quarry. I fell with it, but luckily, not too far. The men ran over to the carcass – I guessed – to collect

the diamonds that had stuck to the skinned carcass, but when I stood up they nearly jumped out of their own skin. However, when I told them of my adventures and, especially, when I shared with them the diamonds I had collected, they were more than happy to assist me. They took me back to their ship and promised to return me to Basra.

'Fate had played with me, taking me from the very edge of despair and then, capriciously, making me rich again. How strange are fate and fortune!'

The Saddle

Themes:
- Invention
- Knowledge and information
- Technology
- The ethics of technology

The story

'And is that the end of your tale?' asked Sindbad the porter.

'If it were, it would be one of the most fantastical tales yet told,' said Sindbad the sailor, 'but fate and fortune had not finished with me yet. I was returned safely home again but it was not long before I was aboard another ship seeking adventure once more. Once a man tastes travel and adventure – and especially fortune – it is a taste not easily given up. The ship, however, was battered by one of the most violent storms I have ever witnessed and was driven towards a rocky outpost. The ship was dashed, as if paper, against the rocks hidden just beneath the surface of the sea. Unlike many of the other sailors I managed to get hold of a piece of flotsam that kept my head above the waves.'

Sindbad continued his story:

'For two days I drifted through the open ocean until I was spotted, against all the odds, by another ship. The men on board were friendly enough and they took me back with them to their own island. When I arrived I was taken to see their king. He invited me to sup with him and to tell him who I was and where I had come from. That evening I began the tale that I have told you. He was so enthralled with my adventures that he asked to hear more the following night. For several nights I entertained the king with my extraordinary tales. I was well looked after.

'I had noticed that the people of this island rode horses as we do at home but that they did not use saddles and bridles.

"Why do you not use saddles?" I asked the king, but it became clear that he did not know what a saddle was. I explained that riding horses is much easier, and more comfortable, with a saddle.

'To show my gratitude for the hospitality shown me by the king I asked if I could offer him, and his people, a gift.

"What could you possibly give me? You have nothing," he observed.

"I will need some leather, some wood, nails and tools. If you can get these for me then I will be able to make *you a gift," I said.*

'He sent for the items I had requested and, immediately, I set to work. I had, as a youth, learned the craft of saddle-making. Though I hadn't made one in a long time, the knowledge had not deserted me, and I was able to make one of the best saddles I had ever made. I showed the king how to use the saddle and bridle and he was overjoyed at the advantages he could see this new technology would afford him and his people.'

Task 1: your gift

TX (see page 7) *Technology:* Suppose that you, like Sindbad, have been lost at sea, then rescued and welcomed by a people that live on an island but without the technological advancements that have been made in your own society. For instance, there are no cars or computers.

Task: Can you think of something that you could introduce to them? Remember: it must be something *you could build or describe how to build* (your suggestions will be tested). Cars or computers are too complicated for us to be able to build or describe in detail. What would you be able to introduce?

First of all, collect ideas from the children, only then, challenge them ('So what would you need to be able to do that?' 'Where would you get nails from? Can you explain how to do that to the blacksmith?'). For example, a class I worked with said:

- an axe
- an elastic band-launcher
- a gun
- a bow and arrow
- a table
- a pencil box.

Next, remove the more complicated / controversial ones (e.g. an elastic band-launcher because it pre-supposes elastic bands; a gun, because it is far too complicated and may be an unsuitable subject for young children). We ended up with:

- an axe
- a bow and arrow

- a table
- a pencil (simplified from 'a pencil box').

Split them into groups. The two questions to ask each group are:

1 What would you need to make it? (Materials, tools etc.)
2 How would you do it? (What instructional steps would be needed?)

Extension activity: instructions

- Set them the task of writing their own set of step-by-step instructions for their item. Test it by asking someone else to follow the instructions.
- Try to explain, by writing it down, how to tie a shoe-lace. Can you do it? Is it easy?
- Can you list ten things that are really very useful, but which are also very simple, such as a paper clip. Can you describe how they are made?

Task 2: would it be right?

The next stage is to move to a moral question. First of all, take an example such as the axe, then ask the class to come up with 'one good thing' about introducing an axe to a society hitherto without axes; then ask for 'one bad thing'. Carry on in this way until you have a reasonably balanced list. One class I did this with came up with (for an axe):

GOOD	BAD
They can chop trees down	They might hurt themselves
Build things	Destroys the environment
Can protect themselves	Children might get hurt

Task Question: Would it be right (or good) to introduce the axe to these people?

Nested Questions:
- Does one outweigh the other? (For example, does the good outweigh the bad?)
- Do long-term considerations outweigh the short-term? What about the other way round?
- How do you decide if something is good or bad for society?
- (The teacher and/or the children could) find out about an approach to ethical / moral considerations such as this, called *consequentialism*. Is consequentialism the right way to make these sorts of decisions?
- Would we be right to interfere with other societies? Would it be wrong not to introduce a technology to another society? What would a consequentialist say? Do you agree?

Extension activity: cars

Cars are thought to be an indispensable item of modern society. Put cars under the same analysis as the axe in the previous activity. Set the class the task of researching the good things and the bad things that cars have conferred on society. Then ask: are cars a good thing or a bad thing for us?

TX car inventor: imagine you went back in time to meet the inventor of the car. Knowing what you know about how cars have impacted on society what would you say to the inventor of cars? Would you try to stop the inventor from inventing cars? (This could be turned into a role-playing exercise, or could be used for the basis of a dialogue – see 'Writing dialogues' on page 116).

The Pit

Themes:
- Cultural relativism
- Customs and practices
- Despair
- The ethics of survival
- Death

The story

Sindbad the sailor continued. He said:

'I made many more saddles and bridles for the most important people of the kingdom and made a great deal of wealth on that island selling more to the people of the island. They welcomed me into their community as an honoured guest and, as was the custom there, I was given a wife. Our wedding was a happy occasion and I stayed on the island for a good deal longer. But, sadly, one day my wife died from an unknown disease. After many days of grief, I was visited by friends, who offered their condolences. Also – though I thought it strange at the time – they said goodbye, as if I were about to leave the island. I could not make out the reason for this behaviour. Then I discovered, to my horror, the meaning of their farewells.

'It was the custom of the people of this island to also bury the living spouse with the dead partner. When I found out what my fate was, I did not meet it calmly. I pleaded with the king not to bury me alive, saying, "I am a foreigner, I do not have to put up with your customs!" But he and the others thought my reaction as odd as I thought their barbaric custom. There was nothing I could do. Two days later, after a ceremonial party – at which I was honoured! – I was lowered into a dark pit with my dead wife, and a heavy lid was placed over us, shutting out all light and the outside world.

'I could not see anything, but quickly realised that I was in an enormous underground tomb. From feeling around with my hands I managed to ascertain that I was surrounded by dead and decomposed bodies of all the husbands and wives that had been buried here before. The fact that I could not see the bodies, but knew they were there, was all the more chilling. To make things worse, I could hear what must have been rats that, from the sound they made, I guessed were large.'

Task Question: Was Sindbad right to object when he said 'I am a foreigner, I do not have to put up with your customs!'?

Nested Questions:
- Should one always respect the laws and / or customs of another society?
- If one should respect the laws / customs of any society then should they respect the laws / customs of Sindbad's society and not impose the custom of spouse burial on him?
- Is it ever right to object to the laws and / or customs of another society?
- Is it ever right to try to change, or interfere, with the laws and / or customs of another society?
- Can you think of something that would be absolutely wrong for any society to adopt as a custom or law? (Classic examples are: torture and suppressing the education of women).
- What do you think of the custom on the island to give honoured guests a wife?
- Are values (morals, laws etc.) relative to different societies?
- Are there any values that are not relative to different societies but which hold for all societies?

(*Suitability warning*: the next section of the story may not be suitable for your class, so make sure that you read ahead to help you make a decision about whether to include Sindbad's killing of another to secure his own survival. If it is not appropriate for your class's age / maturity, then simply omit that part of the narrative; it will not harm the narrative to move directly to the section where he spies the larger animal. In your story (if you are telling it), he may have found a lighting device on the floor, maybe after having fished around among the rats! This sort of editing is easier to do if you are telling the stories rather than reading them. See 'Matching the register' on page 40.)

'*After a few days in the complete darkness I began to feel very weak due to the lack of food and water. A warm tiredness came over me and I was just about to resign myself to being swept away by it, when the lid was moved and daylight streamed into the tomb. Another death had clearly happened and another man was being buried with his dead wife. I was moved into action. The other man had some food and water that I needed. Through great need, delirium and desperation I am ashamed to say that I killed the man to get hold of the sustenance he had on his person.*

'*When I had eaten, some strength returned to me and I discovered that he had a torch and tinderbox. I lit the torch to finally get a good look at my surroundings and see if there was anything that might help with my escape. I* saw the rats that, until now, I had only heard. And they were indeed as big as I'd estimated. But then I caught the glint of an animal's eye, reflecting my light, and it was no rat, being far too large. I saw it vanish behind a rock at the far end of the cave.

'Perhaps, because of the food and water I had managed to get hold of – at great cost to myself! – my mind started to come into focus again. An idea came to me: an animal that size must have got inside the tomb from outside. I quickly ran to where it had vanished behind the rock and followed its only path just as the torch failed. I clambered over rocks for quite some time until eventually a dim light appeared to me in the distance, like a star.

'It kept vanishing behind unseen rocks as I moved towards it until, eventually, I got close enough to see that it was indeed the light from the sun permitted into this dark prison by some merciful aperture in the tomb's natural walls. I hoped and prayed that I would be able to fit through the hole and that I would not find myself arrested again and, perhaps, killed where I stood.

'Though I was bigger than the animal I had seen, I was just able to squeeze through. I fell on to a tiny, stony beach that was hidden on the coast of the island and isolated from any route to it. I was trapped, but at least nobody would come looking for me here.

'After a day of resting there and gathering my thoughts I saw, in the distance, a ship that looked to me that it was passing by the island, not visiting. Ignorant of who manned the ship, where it was going, or whether its crew would be friendly or hostile, I threw myself into the sea and swam, with what strength I could muster, towards it. I knew that the odds were against me, as I was weak and the currents strong. Desperation had already led me to one extreme course of action; now it led me to another.

'I was lucky that someone on board the ship had seen me swimming towards them because, had they not sent some men in a small boat to meet me, I would surely have perished; my strength had deserted me long before I was able to reach my destination. I was dragged out of the water by a sailor and transported back to the ship.

'Though I had survived, a part of me had died. I told my rescuers the story... though only in part.'

N.B. This section only pertains to classes for whom this would be suitable – see suitability warning on page 190.

Task Question: Was Sindbad justified in killing another in order to secure his own survival?

Nested Questions:
- If not 'justified' then can Sindbad be excused? What's the difference between 'justified' and 'excused'?
- Why did he say 'a part of me had died'? And why did he only tell part of his story to his rescuers?
- *TX Cannibal:* Imagine that you were thrown into a situation, like the real-life situation described in the film *Alive*, where the choice was between cannibalism and death. Would it be acceptable to resort to cannibalism? (The class could research the famous case 'Her Majesty The Queen versus Tom Dudley and Edwin Stephens 1884' for the purpose of stimulating a moral / legal discussion.)
- *TX Killer:* Slightly adjust the previous thought-experiment so the choice is between killing another and surviving yourself. Could it ever be justifiable to kill in order to survive?
- Are there any reasons why it might never be justifiable to kill in order to survive?

The Old Man of the Sea

Themes:
- Piety and reward
- Moral motivation
- Self-control
- Addiction
- Hardship
- Slavery
- The ethics of killing

Suitability warning: this story also contains an event that must be considered for suitability. At the end of this story Sindbad beats his persecutor to death with a rock. If you deem it not suitable then either omit the story or adapt it (see 'Adapting to match the register' on page 40). Better to adapt than to miss out a cracking story such as this one.

The story

'The men who had rescued me were on their way to Baghdad but, on their way, they stopped at many islands looking for those to trade with. My journey, therefore, was going to take a great deal longer than I had hoped. One day, the men disembarked on an uninhabited island, and perhaps because of my stories, they were determined to explore it for the possibility of finding their fortune in some strangely fashioned valley or some such thing. I stayed aboard the ship, this time thinking that I would be safer if I did so.

'When the men returned, they began telling of their explorations and of a discovery they claimed to have made. As I heard their story unfold, I heard something that was familiar, but which filled me with a deep unease. They told of how they had seen a dome-shaped building in the distance on the side of a mountain, and they told of how, when they reached it, they couldn't find any doors or windows leading into it.

"What did you do?" I asked, already afraid of the answer they were to give.

"We broke it open with our sabres," they said, "and discovered that it contained a delicious golden food inside not unlike the yolk of an egg."

"That's because it is the yolk of an egg, you fools!" I told them. "And now you will need to flee this island as quickly as possible before the owner of the egg comes looking for you!"

'They did not listen to my pleas and, though they left the island, they were in no rush.

'We had been sailing for a day and I had begun to think that we had escaped the wrath of the roc, whose egg it was.

'I was sleeping below deck when I heard the shouts of the sailors. I came up on deck to see that the ship was cast in shadow, though there was a bright, cloudless sky above. Over us, I saw the gigantic bird that had transported me to the valley of the diamonds, carrying in its talons a huge boulder. At the moment I had looked to see this spectacle, its talons released their grip on the cargo. All we could do was watch as the boulder dropped, with perfect aim, towards the ship's deck. It seemed to me to take forever for the boulder to reach us, as I saw it fall with a slow, dreamlike inevitability.

'The ship was sunk and all those aboard were scattered and lost. I could do nothing other than try to save myself. The Almighty had sent me a piece of flotsam that I hoped would save my life. I managed to haul myself onto it and was able to paddle with my arms. A day's paddling brought me to an island and I stumbled onto the beach wretched, cold and hungry. Once ashore I collapsed, unconscious.

'I awoke and was met by solitude. A little exploring soon told me that I had reached another uninhabited island. "How many uninhabited islands can there be?" I thought. However, the island was far from a desert island; many fruits hung, ripe, from the trees. The fruit nourished me, and for a day and a night, I stayed by the beach doing nothing other than eat as much fruit as I could, but it was not long before I became thirsty; the water from the fruit not sufficient to quench my thirst. I decided to go in search of a freshwater stream or river.

'After walking for an hour or so, I found one, but I also found something else; something very curious indeed. Up until then I had believed the island uninhabited but, sitting still, next to the river, I saw an old man wearing only clothes made of leaves. I tried to speak to him but either he could not, or would not, speak. Though apparently mute, he began to signal with his arms and hands. I worked out from his gesticulations that he was indicating to be carried across the river. The river was not too deep and I thought that if I performed this service for the old man, Allah might reward me and, perhaps, show me a way off the island. I turned around and allowed the old man to climb on to my back then I began to cross the river.'

> **Task Question 1:** What do you think of Sindbad's reason for helping the old man across the river?
>
> Nested Questions:
> - Should we do good deeds for others in order to get rewards for ourselves?
> - Is it right to do good deeds for others for no other reason than because it is a good deed?

'By the time we had reached the other side, however, a very strange thing had happened: as we had crossed the river his legs had begun to wind around my body like two snakes constricting around me, and when I had bent down for him to climb off he dug his leg-snakes into me causing me much pain. I cried out. He started banging me on my ears and yelling at me to go where he wanted to go. I had no choice but to do his bidding, if I was to avoid a great deal of pain and a beating. I cursed and said to myself that I would never do a good deed for another, as long as I lived!'

> **Task Question 2:** What do you think of Sindbad's vow, 'I would never do a good deed for another, as long as I lived!'?
>
> Nested Questions:
> - For what reasons should we do good deeds for others?
> - For what reasons should we stop doing good deeds for others?
> - Should we do good deeds for others? Should we stop?
> - What reasons are there not to do good deeds for others?
> - Does it depend on what happens afterwards?

'The rest of the day, he made me go here and there fetching food and drink for him and travelling all over the island. By the end of the day I was exhausted. When he finally fell asleep I thought that that might be the end of it, but no. Though he slept, his leg-snakes kept their grip on me as if they were independent, living creatures, always awake.

'The next day, from the moment he awoke to when he slept, I was worked without pause. I realised that I was the old man's slave and that I could not escape and, worst of all, that this would not end. Each night, after he had fallen asleep, I had a short time to find some meagre meal for myself before sleep took me – berries and grass, usually. Each day that I grew weaker, the mean old man worked me harder. Every time I disobeyed him he would remind me of the pain he could administer.

'One day, I found some dry gourds (a fleshy, typically large fruit with a hard skin; when dried it can be used as a container) and this gave me an idea. That evening, when the old man slept, I returned to the gourds I had found earlier and cut the tops off of them, then I hollowed them out. Inside, I placed grapes and then replaced the tops. I left the gourds for a few days for the grapes to ferment to make a crude wine.

'When I returned and tasted the wine I found that it was very potent. At the end of each day I would drink some of this concoction to help combat the exhaustion and the despair. It would also help me fall asleep more quickly and deeply. I began to look forward to this time at the end of each day – the feeling the wine afforded being the only thing resembling pleasure in my wretched days.

'One evening, I had been too eager to drink from the gourds and had gone to them too soon – before the old man had fallen asleep. When he saw the effect the wine had on me he said, "What's that you're drinking? Give it to me!" and then he started to beat me around the ears. I gave the gourd to him, crestfallen that even this little pleasure would be denied me from now on. He drank the wine and as it began to affect him he started singing, if singing it be called. He drank more. Then I noticed that, perhaps because of the wine, the vine-like grip his legs had held me in for the past week or so had loosened. Now was my chance! I quickly untangled myself from the old man, who was by now quite drunk, and I flung him to the ground.

'Wasting no time I picked up a rock from the ground and beat him to death. There was no pity to be found in me for the mean old man who had unceasingly treated me as his slave for the last two weeks. I looked at myself: I was only half the man I used to be, so thin and weak had I become. I was incredibly hungry, so I dragged myself to the beach again and feasted as much as I could on the fruit from the trees.

'Eventually, I was picked up by a passing ship that I had been able to signal to, by making a fire and using grass to create smoke. When onboard the ship, I told the crew what had befallen me. They said to me, "Do you know who it was you met? That was the legendary Old Man of The Sea. He is said to entrap lost sailors like yourself and enslave them. It is said that he then works his slave to death before feeding on their dead body. You were lucky to survive, and every sailor will be indebted to you for ridding the world of such an evil parasite." I was rewarded by the sailors with copious amounts of food and drink, but I drank only water.'

This would be an appropriate story to use the Concept Box technique with (see 'The Concept Box' on page 77). However, below are some Task Questions around the main themes.

> **Task Question 3:** The old man of the sea made Sindbad do things he didn't want to do. Can you think of any examples when you do things you don't want to do?
>
> Nested Questions:
> - Do we only do what we want?
> - If you can think of some examples, are those examples in any way like the old man of the sea?
>
> Examples:
> - When you are angry?
> - When teachers or parents tell you to do things?
> - If you are addicted to something? (Such as sugar, caffeine, alcohol or nicotine.)
> - If you act out of duty, such as stopping yourself doing something you shouldn't because you know it is wrong?
> - When you act for the best, such as when you don't eat lots of sweets because you want to enjoy your favourite dinner in the evening?

There was a philosopher called Plato who thought that the human mind has three parts:

1 The thinking part (like the head)
2 The emotional part (like the chest)
3 The wanting part (like the stomach).

> **Task Question 4:** Do you think there are different parts of the mind that want us to do different things?
>
> **Task Question 5a:** Do we always do what we want to do?
>
> **Task Question 5b:** Do we always do what we think is best for us?

The philosopher Socrates thought that *we only do what we think is best for us* (see Plato's Protagoras, Fourth Century BCE) whereas Plato disagreed; he thought that sometimes we are pulled in different directions (see Plato's Republic, Fourth Century BCE). Can you think of an example where you have felt pulled in different directions leaving you both wanting to do something and not wanting to do it?

Task Question 6: Who, if any of these philosophers, do you agree with most?

As with this part of the story, use your judgement about the appropriateness of this discussion (TQ7 below) with your class.

Task Question 7: Was Sindbad justified when he killed The Old Man of The Sea?

Nested Questions:
- When, if ever, is it permissible to kill someone?
- If not justifiable, was it at least understandable, that Sindbad killed the old man?
- What is the difference between *justifiable* and *understandable*?
- Should Sindbad have taken pity on the old man? Why did he feel none?
- What is pity?
- Is revenge ever justified?

This is not a complete account of *The Voyages of Sindbad*. To find out the other adventures that befell him see *The Arabian Nights* (Lyons, Malcolm and Ursula, 2010) for the full account. If you feel so inspired, you could turn some of the other voyages of Sindbad into thinking stories; there are plenty of opportunities to do so as I left many of these stories out for reasons of space as much as anything else. The *Further Voyages of Sindbad* include (with which night the story is told and possible thinking themes in brackets): 'The Black Giant' / Night 546, 'The Magians' / Night 551 (cannibalism), 'The City of The Apes' / Night 558 (imperialism and racism), 'Cinnamon, Pepper and Pearls' / Night 559 (trade), 'The Musk Valley' / Night 560, 'The Underground Stream' / Night 561 (choices / into the unknown), 'The King of Serendib' / Night 562, 'The Region of The Kings' / Night 563 ('there's always a bigger fish!'), 'The Sandalwood Raft' / Night 564, 'The Insect People' / Night 565 and 'The Elephant Graveyard' / Night 566 (ethics of slavery / environmental ethics / animal rights).

Afterword

Sheherazad having beguiled you and having followed Ariadne's thread – this way and that – you have now reached the end of the book and I would like to finish with a cautionary note. Stories can be used well, but stories can also be abused well. Christian Salmon in his book *Storytelling: Bewitching The Modern Mind* (2010) tells us that we are living in an age of storytelling, where institutions and companies no longer rely simply on the power of a product or logo but employ the much more powerfully persuasive medium of narrative, selling not commercials or brands but stories.

Jonathan Douglas, director of The National Literacy Trust, tells us[1] that it is not enough to promote literacy in education; in this time of information – and misinformation – overload, he tells us that children must also be equipped with an activated critical faculty. They need to know how to sift through – how to discern – the good information from the bad and the ugly. I am still shocked by the extent to which children say, 'It's true! I saw it on the internet.' However, I am happy to report that there is always at least one child in each class where this is said who comes back with, 'That doesn't mean it's true.' Literacy is not enough; children need also to develop critical literacy in order to reverse this ratio.

Think or tell?
First, cast the spell!
If think, think well
On the tale you tell.

Peter Worley, 7 October 2013

---

1   Jonathan Douglas said this at a talk he delivered at the LSE: http://www.lse.ac.uk/european Institute/research/forumForEuropeanPhilosophy/events/roundTable/roundTable.aspx

Appendix 1

Quick view steps: how to approach the stories and sessions in this book

Note: this section is intended to act as a reminder only. It is strongly advisable to read the appropriate sections in the book (page numbers are given) to understand how to follow the procedures that are only briefly outlined below.

Basic enquiry procedure

(See 'Enquiry' on page 56.)

An essential part of using stories for thinking is that you must have a method or procedure for conducting a discussion. You may already have one but, if not, here is a quick procedural guide. For a more detailed account of how to conduct a philosophical enquiry (also known as PhiE) see *The If Machine* (page 1–45).

1 *Talking circle*: Sit your class in a circle or horseshoe shape. Eye contact is very important if you want successful discussion-based sessions.

2 *Tell your story*. See 'Sheherazad's handbook' (chapter two) for suggestions of how to do this effectively.

The enquiry section

3 Stop the story at the appropriate time, as indicated in the stories, to run the discussion part of the session. The enquiry part of this procedure is contained within this box.

4 (Optional or alternative) *First Thoughts*: If using this part of the procedure skip step five and go straight to six for their First Thoughts then run the enquiry with no Task Questions.

5 *Task Question (TQ):* Do any necessary set-up, then ask the TQ, writing it up clearly on the board.

6 *Talk Time:* Allow two minutes or so where the children speak to each other in pairs or small groups. Take this opportunity to find out what some individual pairs think.

7 *Gain their attention:* After a couple of minutes of Talk Time use a visual

signal explained at the outset to get the class's attention. I simply put my hand in the air holding the ball that I use for speaker management.

8   *Begin the enquiry:* Remind them of the TQ and begin the enquiry.

9   *Facilitate the enquiry:* Allow as many of the children as possible to speak without insisting, and use the basic strategy of 'anchoring and opening up' or 'if-ing, anchoring and opening up' (see page 74) to facilitate the discussion. But remember *not to say what you think*! Your job is to facilitate a dialogic discussion between the children – one that is built naturally and step-by-step from comments and responses made by the children, leading toward a discussion that is structured, sequential, disciplined and rigorous.

10   *New Task Questions:* If a new TQ emerges from the discussion, or you want to move to a further TQ from the book, then set the new TQ and repeat the process from step three.

11   *Continue, or finish, the story:* If necessary, leave enough time to continue with what's left of the story before moving on to another enquiry in the story or ending the session.

The stories

Here are the main procedures for approaching the majority of the stories in this book.

Emergent Enquiries

(See 'Emergent Questions and Enquiries' on page 59.)

1 Present stimulus (read or tell story). See 'Sheherazad's handbook' (chapter two) for suggestions of how to do this effectively.
2 (Optional) First Thoughts. (See 'First Thoughts' on page 57.)
3 Follow and guide the discussion as it unfolds.
4 Identify a suitable task question from this process (see 'Emergent Questions as Task Questions' on page 60).
5 Write up the question and follow the procedure for running an enquiry. (See 'Basic enquiry procedure' above and 'Enquiry' on page 56.)

Using Task Questions

(See 'Task Questions' on page 58.)

1 Present stimulus (read or tell story). See 'Sheherazad's handbook' (chapter two) for suggestions of how to do this effectively.
2 Either introduce your own task question or follow the plans in the book and set a task question from the appropriate section of the chapter. (You do not need to go through all the enquiry suggestions.)
3 Follow the procedure for running an enquiry. (See 'Basic enquiry procedure' above and 'Enquiry' on page 56.)

Occasionally, such as with the stories *Sindbad and The Island, Sindbad and The Saddle, The Six Wise Men* and *Once Upon an If,* there will be a more involved and specific lesson plan. In this case, read and follow the instructions carefully in that chapter.

The Concept Box

(See 'The Concept Box' on page 77 – for use with any of the stories in this book.)

This is a new procedure, introduced in this book and designed to approach a story or poem conceptually.

1 Present stimulus (read or tell story). See Sheherazad's handbook (chapter two) for suggestions of how to do this effectively.
2 First Thoughts: allow comprehension discussion. (See 'First Thoughts' on page 57.)
3 Concept fishing: collect key concept-words (one from each child, no repetition). *Question: what's the story about?*
4 Concept funnelling: reduce keywords to just five. Questions: *Which word best describes the whole story? Which one best gets to the heart of what the whole story is about?*
5 Exploring concepts: use the chosen key concept-words for your discussion of the stimulus. Have the class explore the concepts in at least some of the following ways:
    • justify ('The story is about X because…')
    • explain ('What I mean by X is…')
    • challenge ('I don't agree that the story is about X because…')
    • analyse ('There are different kinds of X. There is… and there is…')
    • clarify (Teacher: 'Can you say in your own / in different words what is meant by…?')
    • compare ('X is the same as Y because…' / 'X is not the same as Y because…')
    • connect ('X and Y are both kinds of…' / 'X is a type of Y because…')
    • revise ('I think we should take X off the list and replace it with Y because…').

Stories in verse

(See 'Stories in verse' on page 166.)

This is a procedure especially tailored to help you and your class approach the stories in verse in this book. This procedure may also be used with poetry in general.

1 Vocabulary exercise: write unfamiliar words up and figure them out from the context. (See 'Unfamiliar words' on page 166.)
2 Present stimulus (read / recite story). See 'Sheherazad's handbook' (chapter two) for suggestions of how to do this effectively.
3 First Thoughts: comprehension discussion. (See 'First Thoughts' on page 57.)
4 (If necessary) read / recite again leaving out some keywords and phrases for the audience to fill in.
5 Either:
   - Do the Concept Box exercise. (See above and 'The Concept Box' on page 77.)
   - Ask a task question. (See individual story suggested Task Questions (TQs) and see TQs on page 58.)
   - Or follow an Emergent Enquiry. (See 'Emergent Questions and Enquiries' on page 59.)

Once Upon an If (part 1)

Props and preparation needed:

- Two books, a larger one (The Big Story Book) and a smaller one (The Little Story Book).
- Place the smaller book somewhere partly hidden in the classroom, such as under a table or chair.
- (Optional) Wrap the larger book to be unwrapped at the appropriate place in the story.
- Prepare the *Once Upon an If* slide show (log on to the online resources that accompany this book). Show title slide.

Storytelling procedure with slideshow (available online)

1 Read or tell the story *Once Upon an If (part one)*. (Click through slides only where it says to in the text.)
2 Ask Task Questions from the book as you go.
3 Once you finish the story run the story enquiry (see *The Matches* on page 99 with additional suggestions at the end of *Once Upon an If (part one)* on page 91).

Once Upon an If (part 2)

1 Recap *Once Upon an If (part one)*.
2 Read *Matilda, The Fireless Dragon*.
3 Ask Task Questions from the book as you go to engage the class in creative thinking and story-problem solving.
4 Finish the story.

Once Upon an If classroom activity

1 *Story partner*: Pair-up each member of the class with a 'story partner'.
2 *The Little Story Book:* Have everyone complete the content part of the exercise. Use The Little Story Book template provided (see page 215) and have everyone fill it out for their partner.
3 *Swap Little Story Books*: Have each pair swap the completed Little Story Book template with each other.
4 *The Big Story Book*: Each pupil should then write a story, making use of, and adhering to, the information provided by their story partner. 'What would your story do?' / 'What would that character do?' – they should try to stay true to their story partner's ideas. They are permitted to change the story ideas only with good narrative reasons. Use the story mountain (see pages 218 and 219 and Appendix 3) to help structure the stories.
5 *Swap Big Story Books*: Have each pair swap their stories, once written, so they can now, like Zadie, read the story that has been written and that waits to be discovered.
6 (Optional) They could write a short review of the story, commenting on whether the story has remained true to their original ideas and whether it was an interesting and / or exciting interpretation of their ideas.

More stories to think with

How to approach stories not in this book (see www.philosophy-foundation.
org/resources for more stories to think with).

Decide whether you are going to read or tell the story. Hopefully, after reading
Once Upon an If, you will want to at least try some storytelling. If you opt to
tell then:

- (Optionally) research versions of the story.
- (And / or) read the story and make a keyword list (see 'Keyword lists' on
  page 35).

Whether you tell or read:

- Decide what your aims and objectives are and devise questions for the story to
  meet them (see 'Finding the right question' on page 59).
- Alternatively, use First Thoughts and follow an Emergent Enquiry (see 'First
  Thoughts' on page 57 and 'Emergent Questions and Enquiries' on page 59)
  or use a method such as the Concept Box (see 'The Concept Box' on
  page 77).
- Decide where, in the story, to put your questions for your enquiries (see 'When
  to ask a question' on page 63).

Appendix 2

The Little Story Book – story-writing template

For the writing activity following *Once Upon an If (part one)* and *Matilda, The Fireless Dragon*, see page 97. (Also available online for interactive whiteboard projection.)

Who?   (Who is the main character or characters?)
            Write here…

What?   (What they are, for example, dragon or rabbit and so on? Are there any significant objects such as a magical ring that will be needed to execute your idea?)

Where?   (Is it in any particular place, such as a castle, city or school?)

When?   (Is it in any particular time, such as the past, the present or the future? If so, then what particular past? Middle ages, 18th Century, yesterday?)

What if?   (What is the special event, device or difference that makes it different from the everyday world?)

Who else?   (What other characters are there, or do there need to be, to execute your idea?)

Problem: (What problem is faced by your character or characters?)

Resolution: (How is the problem going to be solved, if at all?)

Genre: (Is your story a science fiction story, a horror story, a fairy tale, or some other genre? Maybe you can create your own genre.)

Example: *Matilda, The Fireless Dragon*

Who?   Matilda.

What?   A dragon.

Where?   Fairy Tale Land.

When?   Once upon a time…

What if?   There was a dragon that could not breathe fire.

Who else?   A king and queen; an annoying knight; a teenager princess; a water monster.

Problem: Matilda has to repel the water monster though she has no fire breath.

Resolution: She bluffs the water monster into leaving the town.

Genre: Fairy Tale.

Story mountain

(See page 220 for diagram.)

Beginning:　(How will you introduce your main character, supporting characters and their significant character traits?)

Build up:　(What will happen to bring about the circumstances of your problem? What clues can you provide for later events?)

Problem:　(What problem or dilemma will face your characters and how will it be introduced in a convincing way?)

Resolution:　(What will happen to bring about a resolution to your problem or dilemma?)

Ending:　(How will you end your story? Will it be a happy ever after or a dark unresolved story, or will it have a twist?)

Example story mountain: *Matilda, The Fireless Dragon*

Beginning: Matilda is introduced. She can't breathe fire and she wants to be alone.

Build up: Princess chains herself to cave and the knight tries to slay Matilda.

Problem: Water elemental monster terrorises town, Matilda is enlisted to help but she is unable to breathe fire and the knight tells the monster so.

Resolution: Matilda employs a psychological trick, based on bluff, to frighten the monster away.

Ending: The monster leaves and Matilda is the hero. She eats the knight. The princess moves in – not quite a happily ever after.

Appendix 3

Story mountain and extension activities

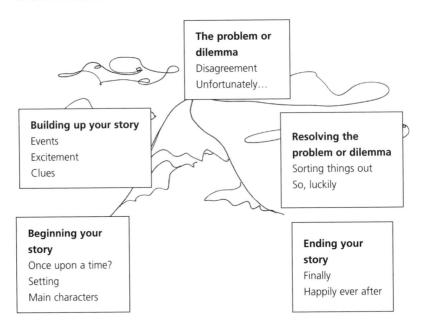

The problem or dilemma
Disagreement
Unfortunately…

Building up your story
Events
Excitement
Clues

Resolving the problem or dilemma
Sorting things out
So, luckily

Beginning your story
Once upon a time?
Setting
Main characters

Ending your story
Finally
Happily ever after

This should be used for the second part of the *Once Upon an If* story-writing activity (see page 97). Once the children have been handed their *who?, what?, where?, when?, what if?* and *who else?* list they might want to use this structure in order to write the story. However, some children may want to subvert this story structure in some way. You may want to encourage this. Alternatively, particularly if you are running the activity for a second time, you may want to adhere to the structure the first time and then invite them to experiment with it for the second. For instance, they may choose to end the story without necessarily resolving the problem (see *The Luckiest Man in the World* on page 177) or they may want to introduce characters in a way that raises more questions (see *It* on page 147). It is important for the children to use the story mountain as a point of departure as much as a model to be followed. For an example of using the story mountain see Appendix 2 'Story mountain' on page 218.

Extension activity

Can the children fill in the story mountain with *The Boy With No Name?* (This story was written explicitly around the story mountain structure.)

Beginning: Boy believes he has lost his name.

Build up: He goes in search of it and meets some other characters, each with their own special relationship to their name.

Problem: He is informed that you cannot lose a name, but that he must never have had one.

Resolution: He meets a girl whose name is too long. He helps her by shortening hers and, at the same time, finding a name for himself.

Ending: He goes home and is able to respond to his mum's question, 'Who is it?' with 'Bob'.

References, bibliography and recommended resources

Storytelling

Baker, Augusta and Greene, Ellin (1977), *Storytelling: Art and Technique*. New York: R. R. Bowker Co.

Breneman, L. and Breneman, B. (1983), *Once Upon a Time: A Storytelling Handbook*. Chicago: Nelson-Hall.

Egan, Kieran (1989), *Teaching as Storytelling*. University of Chicago Press.

Livo, Norma J. and Rietz, Sandra (1986), *Storytelling Process and Practice*. Littleton, CO: Libraries Unlimited.

MacDonald, Margaret Read (1982), *The Storyteller's Sourcebook: A Subject, Title, and Motif Index to Folklore Collections for Children*. Detroit, Michigan: Neal-Schuman Publishers, Inc.

MacDonald, Margaret Read (1993), *The Storyteller's Start-up Book: Finding Learning, Performing and Using Folktales*. New York: August House /H.W. Wilson Co.

Nesbitt, Elizabeth (January February 1940), 'Hold on to that which is good,' *The Horn Book Magazine*.

Sawyer, Ruth. (1942), *The Way of the Storyteller*. New York: Viking Press.

SfS (Society for Storytelling): http://www.sfs.org.uk/

Shedlock, Marie. (1915, reprinted 1951), *The Art of the Storyteller*. NY: Dover Publications, Inc. (Kindle edition)

Sheppard, Tim. *http://www.timsheppard.co.uk/main.html*

Sierra, Judy (1996), *Storytellers' Research Guide*. Oregon: Folkprint.

DVDs and television programmes

Bronowski, Jacob (1973), *The Ascent of Man*. (DVD)

BBC 4 (2012), *The Two Thousand Year Old Computer*. (DVD)

Cbeebies: *Magic Hands* and *Old Jack's Boat* with Bernard Cribbins.

Channel 4/PBS (2005), *Leonardo's Dream Machines*. (DVD)

Groening, Matt (1989), *The Simpsons*.

Henson, Jim (1988), *Jim Henson's Storyteller* with John Hurt. (DVD)

The poet and playwright Simon Armitage has translated acclaimed versions of Homer's *Odyssey* (2007), Faber & Faber, and *Sir Gawain and The Green Knight* (2009), Faber & Faber, and is a master storyteller. Many of his documentaries for television and radio are great examples of how storytelling can be used effectively with non-fiction. See in particular *The Pendle Witch Child* (BBC 4, 2011).

The Storyspinner. http://thestoryspinner.co.uk/

Story collections

Abrahams, Roger D. (1983), *African Folktales*. Pantheon Books.

Aesop. *Aesop's Fables*. Many editions.

Alderson, Brian and Foreman, Michael (1992), *The Arabian Nights or Tales Told by Sheherazade During a Thousand Nights and One Night*. Gollancz.

Borges, J.L. (2000), *Labyrinths*. Penguin.

Brunvand, Jan Harold (2001), *Too Good To Be True: The Colossal Book of Urban Legends*. W. W. Norton & Co. New edition.

Calvino, Italo (1981), *Italian Folktales*. Pantheon Books.

Cam, Philip (1998). *Thinking Stories 1*. Hale and Iremonger Pty. Ltd.

Cam, Philip (1998), *Thinking Stories 2*. Hale and Iremonger Pty. Ltd.

Carter, Angela (1991), *The Virago Book of Fairytales*. Virago Press Ltd.

Coe, Fanny E. (1914 Kindle edition), *The Book of Stories For The Story-Teller*.

Fisher, Robert (1999), *First Stories for Thinking*. Nash Pollock Publishing.

Fisher, Robert (1996), *Stories for Thinking*. Nash Pollock Publishing.

Fisher, Robert (1997), *Values for Thinking*. Nash Pollock Publishing.

Fleetham, Mike (2007), *Thinking Stories to Wake Up Your Mind*. LDA.

Forest, Heather (2011), *Wisdom Tales from Around the World*. August House Publishing.

Garner, Alan (2011), *Collected Folk Tales*. Harper Collins.

Graves, Robert (2011), *The Greek Myths*. Penguin re-issue.

Grayling, A.C. (ed.) (2011), 'Parables' and 'Histories' in *The Good Book*. Bloomsbury.

Gunn, James *The Road To Science Fiction*. (6 Volumes), Scarecrow Press.

Herodotus (circa 430 BCE) *Histories*. Many editions.

Homer. *The Iliad* and *The Odyssey*. Many editions.

Littleton, Scott C. (New edition 2004), *Mythology: The Illustrated Anthology*. Duncan Baird Publishers.

Lyons, Malcolm and Ursula (2010), *The Arabian Nights: Tales of 1001 Nights Vols.1-3*. Penguin.

March, Jenny (1999), *Dictionary of Classical Mythology*. Orion.

McCaughrean, Geraldine (1992), *The Orchard Book of Greek Myths*. Orchard Books.

McCaughrean, Geraldine (2001), *100 World Myths and Legends*. Orion.

Rackham, Arthur (illustrator) (1994). *English Fairy Tales*. Wordsworth.

Tatar, Maria (Expanded edition 2012), *The Annotated Brothers Grimm*. W. W. Norton & Co.

Tatar, Maria (2002), *The Annotated Classic Fairy Tales*. BCA.

Thomas, Taffy and Killick, Steve (2007), *Telling Tales: Storytelling as Emotional Literacy*. Educational Printing Services Ltd.

Yolen, Jane. (1987), *Favorite Folktales from Around the World*. Pantheon: NewYork.

Thought-experiments

Baggini, Julian (2010), *The Pig That Wants To Be Eaten and Ninety Nine Other Thought Experiments*. Granta Books.

Cave, Peter (2007), *Can A Robot Be Human? 33 Perplexing Philosophy Puzzles*. One World Publications.

Cave, Peter (2010), *Do Llamas Fall In Love? 33 Perplexing Philosophy Puzzles*. One World Publications.

Cave, Peter (2009), *This Sentence Is False An Introduction To Philosophical Paradoxes*. One World Publications. Continuum International Group Ltd.

Cave, Peter (2008), *What's Wrong With Eating People? 33 More Perplexing Philosophy Puzzles*. One World Publications.

Cohen, Martin (2004), *Wittgenstein's Beetle And Other Classic Thought Experiments*. Wiley-Blackwell.

Cohen, Martin. (1999, 2000, 2002), *101 Philosophy Problems*. Routledge.

Cohen, Martin (2003), *101 Ethical Dilemmas*. Routledge.

Tittle, Peg (2004), *What If...?* Collected Thought Experiments in Philosophy. Pearson.

Worley, Peter (ed.) (2012), *The Philosophy Shop*. Crown House.

Philosophy books, papers and websites

Al Ghazali (Eleventh Century), *The Incoherence of The Philosophers*. Many editions.

Anscombe, G.E.M. (second edition 2000), *Intention*. Section 3–4 p.7 Harvard University Press.

Ariew, Roger and Garber, Daniel (1989), *G.W. Leibniz: Philosophical Essays*. Hackett.

Aristotle (Fourth Century BCE), *Metaphysics*. Many editions.

Avicenna (Twelfth Century), *The Book of The Soul*. Many editions.

Benjamin, Walter (1999), 'The Storyteller' in *Illuminations*. Pimlico.

Berkeley, George (1713), *Three Dialogues Between Hylas and Philonus*. Many editions.

Comte-Sponville, Andre (2002), *A Short Treatise On The Great Virtues*. Picador.

Curley, Edwin M. (1994), *A Spinoza Reader: The Ethics and Other Works*. Princeton University Press.

Currie, Gregory (2012), *Narratives and Narrators: A Philosophy of Stories*. OUP Oxford.

Descartes, Rene (1641), *Meditations on The First Philosophy*. Various editions.

Frankfurt, Harry G. 'Freedom of The Will and The Concept of a Person' in *The Journal of Philosophy* Vol. 68 no. 1.

Hume, David (1748), *An Enquiry Concerning Human Understanding*. Many editions.

Hume, David (1739), *A Treatise of Human Nature*. Many editions.

Hume, David (1779), *Dialogues Concerning Natural Religions*. Many editions.

McCabe, Mary Margaret (2006), 'Is Dialectic as Dialectic Does? The Virtue of Philosophical Conversation' in *The Virtuous Life in Greek Ethics* edited by Burkhard Reis. Cambridge University Press.

Montaigne, Michel de. (1580), Essays: *On The Art of Conversation*. Many editions.

Nussbaum, Martha (1990), *Love's Knowledge, Essays on Philosophy and Literature*. New York, Oxford University Press.

Plato (Fourth Century BCE), *Meno*. Many editions.

Plato (Fourth Century BCE), *Protagoras*. Many editions.

Plato (Fourth Century BCE), *Republic*. Many editions.

Plato (Fourth Century BCE), *Theaetetus*. Many editions.

Salmon, Christian (2010), *Storytelling: Bewitching The Modern Mind*. Verso.

Schopenhauer, Arthur (1839), Prize Essay *On The Freedom of The Will*. Many editions.

Strawson, Peter (1966), 'Self, Mind and Body' in *Common Factor* vol. 4.

Williams, Bernard (2009), 'Life As Narrative' in *European Journal of Philosophy* Vol. 17 issue 2.

www.philosophy-foundation.org/resources

http://plato.stanford.edu/entries/holes/

Philosophy in schools (P4C)

Day, Andrew and Worley, Peter (2012), *Thoughtings: Puzzles, Problems and Paradoxes in Poetry to Think With.* Crown House.

Fisher, Robert (2000), *First Poems for Thinking.* Nash Pollock Publishing.

Fisher, Robert (1997), *Games for Thinking.* Nash Pollock Publishing.

Fisher, Robert (1997), *Poems for Thinking.* Nash Pollock Publishing.

Fisher, Robert (1998, 2003, 2004), *Teaching Thinking.* Continuum.

Gaut, Berys and Gaut, Morag (2011), *Philosophy for Young Children a Practical Guide.* Taylor and Francis.

Gopnik, Alison (2009), *The Philosophical Baby.* Farrar, Straus and Giroux.

Haynes, Joanna and Murris, Karin (2012), *Picture Books, Pedagogy and Philosophy*, Routledge.

Law, Stephen (2011), *The Complete Philosophy Files.* Orion Children's.

Law, Stephen (2004), *The Philosophy Gym.* Headline Review.

Wartenberg, Thomas E. (2013), *A Sneetch Is a Sneetch.* Wiley-Blackwell.

Wartenberg, Thomas E. (2009), *Big Ideas for Little Kids.* Rowman & Littlefield Education.

Worley, Peter (2011) *The If Machine: Philosophical Enquiry in the Classroom.* Continuum.

Worley, Peter (2012), *The If Odyssey: A Philosophical Journey through Greek Myth and Storytelling for 8-to-16-year-olds.* Bloomsbury Education.

Worley, Peter (ed.) (2012), *The Philosophy Shop.* Crown House.

Worley, Peter. (2013), 'The Question X' in *Creative Teaching and Learning.* Vol. 4.1. Available here: http://www.philosophy-foundation.org/media-centre/media-coverage-archive

Stories and writing

Cox, Ailsa (2005), *Writing Short Stories.* Routledge.

Haven, Kendall (2007), *Story Proof: The Science Behind The Startling Power of Story.* Libraries Unlimited Inc.

Hohn, Max T. (1943) *Stories in Verse.* Bobbs-Merrill Company Inc.

Madden, Matt (2006), *99 ways to tell a story: exercises in style.* Jonathan Cape.

McCloud, Scott (1994), *Understanding Comics.* Harper Collins.

Orwell, George (1946), 'Politics and The English Language' in *Essays.* Penguin Classics.

Queneau, Raymond (2008), *Exercises in style.* Oneworld Classics Ltd.

Tolkien, J.R.R. (2009), *Tree and Leaf.* Harper Collins.

Truss, Lynne (2009), *Eats, Shoots and Leaves.* Fourth Estate.

Stories in verse (or narrative poetry)

As well as those titles listed below, all of the stories by Julie Donaldson are good examples of stories in verse.

Ahlberg, Allan (1989), *The Mighty Slide.* Puffin.

Browning, Robert (1842), *The Pied Piper of Hamlyn.* Many editions.

Dahl, Roald (2012), *Revolting Rhymes.* Jonathan Cape.

Hohn, Max T. (1943) *Stories In Verse.* Bobbs-Merrill Company, Inc.

Milligan, Spike (1999). *A Children's Treasury of Milligan.* Virgin Books.

Noyes, Alfred and Keeping, Charles (illustrator) (1999), *The Highwayman*. Oxford University Press.

Silverstein, Shel (1969), *A Boy Named Sue*. (A hit for country singer Johnny Cash)

Tennyson, Alfred Lord and Keeping, Charles (illustrator) (1999), *The Lady of Shallot*. Oxford University Press.

For more narrative poems see these sites:

http://en.wikipedia.org/wiki/Narrative_poetry

http://www.lancsngfl.ac.uk/curriculum/literacy/lit_site/html/fiction/narrative/

http://www.blackcatpoems.com/n/narrative_poems.html

Miscellaneous

Blind men and an elephant: http://en.wikipedia.org/wiki/Blind_men_and_an_elephant Hemingway short story and shortest joke:

http://www.bitcomedy.co.uk/classic-comedy/the-worlds-shortest-joke/

Bate, Jonathan ed. (2005), *Andrew Marvell: The Complete Poems*. Penguin Classics.

Baum, L. Frank (1900), *The Wizard of Oz*. Various editions.

Brown, Anthony (2009), *Little Beauty*. Walker Books.

Brown, Margaret Wise (1949), *The Important Book*. Harper Collins.

Carroll, Noel and Hunt, Lester (eds) (2009), *Philosophy in The Twilight Zone*. Wiley-Blackwell.

Conrad, Joseph (1899), *Heart of Darkness*. Various editions.

Copi, Irving M. and Cohen, Carl (2008), *Introduction to Logic*. Prentice Hall.

Dahl, Roald (1979), *Tales of The Unexpected*. Penguin.

Dick, Philip K. (1987, 1988, 1989, 1990, 1991, 2010, 2011, 2012, 2013) *The Collected Stories of Philip K. Dick, Vols. 1–5*. Underwood-Miller; Gollancz; Citadel Twilight; Subterranean Press.

Diet of Worms:

http://www.britannica.com/EBchecked/topic/649151/Diet-of-Worms

http://en.wikipedia.org/wiki/Martin_Luther#Diet_of_Worms

Goffman, Erving (1981), *Forms of Talk*. University of Pennsylvania Press.

Goodman, Nelson (1990), *Fact, Fiction and Forecast*. Harvard University Press.

Hargreaves, Roger (2008), *Mr Good*. Egmont Books Ltd.

Jackson, Steve and Livingstone, Ian (2003), *Fighting Fantasy Boxset: Gamebooks 1–8*. Wizard Books.

Jacobs, W.W. (1902), *The Monkey's Paw*. Many editions.

Johnstone, Keith (2007), *Impro*. Methuen.

Johnstone, Keith (1999), *Impro for Storytellers*. Faber and Faber.

Kitamura, Satoshi (2007), *UFO Diary*. Andersen Press.

Kurosawa, Akira (1950), *Rashomon* (film).

Maguire, Gregory (1995), *Wicked: The Life and Times of The Wicked Witch of The West*. Harper.

Maupassant, Guy de. (1884), *The Necklace*. Many editions.

McKee, David (1980), *Not Now, Bernard*. Red Fox.

Milne, A.A. (1926), *Winnie-The-Pooh*. Methuen.

Milne, A.A. (1928), *The House At Pooh Corner*. Methuen.

Ness, Patrick (2012), *A Monster Calls*. Walker Books.

Nolen, Christopher (2000), *Memento*.

Pfister, Marcus (1992), *The Rainbow Fish*. North South.

Pinter, Harold (1978), *Betrayal*. Faber and Faber.

Poe, Edgar Allan (1841), *The Murders in The Rue Morgue*. Many editions.

Poe, Edgar Allan (1846), *The Cask of Amontillado*. Many editions.

Poe, Edgar Allan (1842), *The Pit and The Pendulum*. Many editions.

Potter, Beatrix (1909), *The Tale of The Flopsy Bunnies*. F. Warne and co.

Pratchett, Terry (with Ian Stewart and Jack Cohen) (2013), *The Science of Discworld 2: The Globe*. Ebury Press.

Shelley, Mary (1818), *Frankenstein, or The Modern Prometheus*. Many editions.

Steig, William (1990), *Shrek*. Particular Books.

Suvin, Darko (1979), *Metamorphoses of Science Fiction: On The Poetics and History of a Poetic Genre*. Yale University Press.

Tarantino, Quentin (1994), *Pulp Fiction*.

Tolkien, J.R.R. (1937), *The Hobbit, or There and Back Again*. George Allen and Unwin.

Very Short Stories (six words long!): http://www.wired.com/wired/archive/14.11/sixwords.html

Velthuijs, Max (1997), *Frog is a Hero*. Andersen.

Watterson, Bill (1995), *The Essential Calvin & Hobbes: A Calvin and Hobbes Treasury*. Sphere.

Wells, H.G. (1895), *The Time Machine*. Various editions.

Willems, Mo (2005), *Knuffle Bunny: A Cautionary Tale*. Walker Books.

Wormell, Chris (2008), *The Saddest King*. Red Fox Picture Books.